W9-BEF-140

A GARDEN STYLE BOOK

EASY ROSES

OLD AND NEW

[SIMPLE SECRETS FOR GLORIOUS GARDENS—INDOORS AND OUT]

GEORGEANNE BRENNAN
PHOTOGRAPHY BY FAITH ECHTERMEYER

CHRONICLE BOOKS

SAN FRANCISCO

Text copyright © 1995 by Georgeanne Brennan.
Photographs copyright © 1995 by Faith Echtermeyer.
All rights reserved. No part of this book may be
reproduced in any form without written
permission from the publisher.

Library of Congress Cataloging-in-Publication Data
Brennan, Georgeanne, 1943–
Easy roses: simple secrets for glorious gardens,
indoors and out/by Georgeanne Brennan; photography
by Faith Echtermeyer.
     p.   cm.
"A Garden Style Book."
Includes bibliographical references (p. 106) and index.
ISBN 0-8118-0749-5
1. Roses. 2. Rose culture. I. Title.
SB411.B75 1995
635.9'33372–dc20   94-13123
                        CIP

Printed in Hong Kong

ISBN 0-8118-0749-5

Cover and interior design by
Aufuldish & Warinner

Distributed in Canada by Raincoast Books,
8680 Cambie Street, Vancouver, B.C. V6P 6M9

10 9 8 7 6 5 4 3 2 1

Chronicle Books
275 Fifth Street
San Francisco, CA 94103

To Jim and Charlotte. −G. B.

Contents

CONTAINER ROSES FOR WINDOWSILLS OR FIRE ESCAPES 42

CONTAINER ROSES FOR BALCONIES AND PATIOS 52

ROSES FOR SMALL GARDEN SPACES 62

Introduction

ew gardening experiences are as dramatic and as fulfilling as growing roses. Cutting a basket or bucketful of unfolding buds and lush blooms from your own garden is a genuine triumph, and rose-growing, which at times may seem elusive, difficult, and fraught with failure, can readily be this successful. The world is full of roses that are easy to grow, will grow in containers and small spaces, and are glorious climbers, ground covers, hedges, or standalone bushes. In all the plant world they offer the greatest variety of sensory pleasures.

¶From my earliest years, I developed the idea that the growing of roses was an arcane and mysterious business practiced only by adept initiates. I had great friendships with many adults in the extended neighborhood in the small Southern California beach town where I grew up who raised roses in their front yards. We conversed while I sat on the curb and my friends—many of whom were retired or had no apparent job—did something to their rosebushes. The rosebushes seemed to be a source of worry

and concern to my friends. There was much snipping and cutting, powdering and spraying, digging and special watering done, but no one ever enthused about the flowers or cut me a rose to take home from those stiff, unfriendly bushes.

¶The romance of the rose was revealed to me not in the gardens I saw but in fairy tales, history, and movies. For years I dreamed of discovering "the black rose" as I galloped on horseback across Turkey and Afghanistan, mentally reenacting the scenes from the movie named for it. The monstrous thorny hedge that engulfed Sleeping Beauty's castle enchanted me, and I could easily imagine popping down a rabbit hole like Alice and chatting with the full-faced roses depicted in my copy of Through the Looking Glass. As an adolescent I pondered the meaning of the Little Prince's conversation with his thorny, bossy, prima donna of a rose. I tried to visualize roses so wondrous that in medieval England they symbolized a noble house and gave name to a war. In Shakespeare's plays I found roses climbing bowers and balconies, and happily for me, when I first traveled to Europe as a student I saw the roses that thus far I had only imagined. Later I learned that many of them were "old" roses and that the roses I had grown up with were mostly modern roses of the hybrid tea types.

¶ The vast spectrum of rose types now commercially available especially encourages novice rose growers. Descriptions for some of the older roses such as "needs little or no pruning," "vigorous," "hardy," and "thrives in almost every climate" animate a gardener with enthusiasm and hope of success, and rightly so.

¶ There are literally thousands of named roses, each with a coterie of devotees, and in such a small book as this only the tiniest fraction can be presented. And I confess, the roses chosen for this book are easy-to-grow favorites of mine and not at all an impartial list. A number of commercial rose growers, amateurs, old rose-hands, breeders, and enthusiasts have shared their technical knowledge and anecdotal experiences with me. This shared, personal aspect of rose growing is so rich that, for me, much of the fun is the talking with people who grow roses, the exchanged cuttings, and the visits to rose gardens, as well as reading the history of what I see. Yet even those enjoyments pale beside the experience of cutting roses I myself have grown.

¶By choosing varieties of roses that are appropriate to one's climate and space restrictions, anyone can grow roses successfully. There exists among rose lovers a camaraderie that encourages asking questions about how best to grow a particular variety, treat a disease, or identify a rose. In working on this book the sense of community and lore in which rose lovers delight has become even more apparent to me. Rose-growing, like other gardening, should be pursued with a sense of adventure, flexibility, and above all, pleasure.

Species, old, and modern roses

The literature of roses is enormous, and numerous tomes explore them in fine and fascinating detail. The purpose here is to provide a brief description of the categories of roses and their characteristics, to help you choose those that interest you and to assist you when buying and planting a rose. Roses can be categorized generally as species, old, or modern.

¶Species roses, to put it simply, are wild roses, and they occur over the northern hemisphere from the frigid and seemingly barren tundras and tiogas of Canada, Russia, and China to the warm Mediterranean basin and the subtropics of Mexico. They have numerous growing forms. Some are ramblers, sending out long canes that may reach upward forty feet and more and spread a hundred feet, while others are smallish shrubs. In between the two extremes are countless other forms.

¶Some of the species roses flower only once during the year, and others flower repeatedly over a period of several months. Colors vary from brilliant crimson and yellow to soft pinks, creams, roses, and shocking magenta. Species roses have hybridized in nature as well as under the human hand, and thus we have the expression "species roses and their hybrids."

¶The lore of the wild roses reaches us from the mists of time, from the ancient world and even Arthurian legend, and it continues to spin today. Only recently Martyn Rix, the well-known English botanist and rosarian, traveled to China with photographer and author Roger Phillips to track and record the four great wild stud roses that origi-nally were brought from China to the west and are thought to be the parents of many of the modern roses.

¶Although wild roses are clearly old, the term "old rose" has a specific meaning in rose nomenclature. Old roses are generally considered to be those garden roses whose breeding and cultivation predates that of the first hybrid tea rose in 1867. Some of the old roses are very old indeed. Gallicas and damasks date back to the gardens of ancient Rome and Persia. Tender repeat-blooming China roses adorned Oriental gardens for more than two thousand years before the first one was introduced in Europe in 1792. A number of these very old roses are still readily available to us, as are those that were bred in Europe, particularly in France, during the eighteenth and nineteenth centuries. Examples are centifolias, with full double flowers that make heavy, bending heads; the lovely moss roses, whose canes and buds are covered with furred, soft "moss"; and the hybrid perpetuals, free flowering and lush looking. As with species roses, many of the old roses bloom only once during late spring or early summer, though others are repeat bloomers. The general shape of the blooms of old roses may be thought of as flat, or "cupped," and "quartered," that is, the petals are organized in quadrants within the bloom, and with "buttons" in the center. The colors of the old roses are primarily varia-tions of pink, magenta, and white. The growth habits of the old roses vary, but generally speaking they are looser, larger, and more open in form than the hybrid teas of the mod-ern period. Sizes and shapes of the old rose varieties vary from three-foot shrubs to mounding specimens six feet and more high and as wide, and include climbers as well.

¶Modern roses are considered to be those whose breeding reflects the crosses made to create the hybrid tea. When a China tea rose was crossed with a hybrid perpetual in 1867, the results were to be access to an entire new range of colors in garden roses, what is called an elegance of form, and repeat flowering. The oranges, yellows, deep reds, and color variations thereof, which ensued with further breeding and are now common, revolutionized the world of roses. When the species rose *R. foetida persiana* was successfully crossed with a hybrid tea, the color yellow was introduced to modern roses. The high-pointed buds and comely plant shapes of the hybrid teas set the standards for rose beauty for the next hundred years, during which there was an enormous amount of breeding. The result has been the grand spectrum of the modern or twentieth-century roses, almost all of them repeat bloomers. They include the floribundas and grandifloras—hybrid tea crosses with numbers of large flowers clustered together on each single stem—and the modern shrub roses and climbers, miniature roses, and landscape or ground-cover roses.

¶In the 1960s another revolution occurred. David Austin, a master rose breeder in England, introduced yet another new type, the English roses. These have the flower forms, shapes, and fragrance associated with old roses but have the repeat bloom, color range, and smaller, more compact size associated with modern roses.

¶Roses of every type make exhilarating cut flowers. Not only is there huge variety among roses in the shape and color of the flowers, there is near-infinite variation of the shapes and colors of the leaves, stems, thorns, and ultimately the hips, also called heps, or seed pods, especially in the species and old roses. For years, the long-stemmed,

hothouse-grown, tightly budded hybrid tea roses have dominated the floral trade, and consequently have dictated our concept of what constitutes roses as cut flowers. Recently, though, trend-setting floral designers have been demanding natural looking roses, primarily modern roses such as floribundas and hybrid teas, but also some of the old and species types, that have been grown not in hothouses but in fields and gardens. Thus the term "garden rose" has come to mean, in common parlance, any rose not hothouse grown.

¶Of course, home gardeners have at their fingertips the kind of garden bounty and variety that are the dreams of floral designers. We have only to reach into our gardens, no matter how small or large, to find a perfect bud, a full-blown blossom, or a cluster of shiny red hips.

¶I debated how closely to differentiate roses and their categories in so small a book, because the subject is both huge and labyrinthine. In the end, it seemed that a brief overview would be background for the roses selected for this book, and would provide a basis for your selecting other roses you might wish to grow. Please keep in mind that the color of a rose and the size of the plant will vary to some extent depending upon the climate and conditions in which it is grown.

SPECIES ROSES

The species roses are among the most pest- and disease-free of all the roses, as well as being vigorous. Some are small, but most are larger shrubs. There are close to two hundred species roses, plus their hybrids, and their interrelationships can be confusing. For example, *Rosa gallica* is a species rose and "gallica rose," which can refer to *Rosa gallica*, describes not only that rose but a category of numerous rose varieties. A number of mail-order catalogues offer some species roses, and some nurseries carry a selection as well. These are some of the best known plus personal favorites.

¶*Rosa banksiae* 'Alba' is a rambler that grows to sixty feet or more high and spreads as wide, with clusters of small, double white flowers. Once-blooming, fragrant, and hardy.

¶*Rosa banksiae* 'Lutea' is, like the 'Alba' above, a rambler that grows to sixty feet or more high and spreads as wide, with clusters of small, double flowers that are pale yellow. Once-blooming and fragrant; hardy, but less so than *R. banksiae* 'Alba'.

¶*Rosa foetida* 'Bicolor', also called Austrian Copper, is a shrub that grows to ten feet with single small flowers. The flower petals are yellow inside and heavily tinged with reddish orange outside. Once-blooming, and somewhat fragrant, this is a hardy rose.

¶*Rosa gallica* has large pink, single-petaled flowers. A smallish shrub growing to three feet and spreading, it is extremely fragrant and is the ancestor of many of the fragrant old garden roses. It is repeat blooming and hardy.

¶*Rosa moyesii* is a moderately thorny shrub that grows to twenty feet and spreads. It has small, single red to pink flowers followed by deep-red urn-shaped hips $2\frac{1}{2}$ inches long. It is once-flowering and somewhat fragrant.

¶*Rosa roxburghii* is also called the chestnut rose or burr rose because of its round, prickly fruit. Native to western China and Japan, this angular shrub grows to ten feet and has fragrant pink flowers, which bloom throughout summer. Small, delicate leaves grow in clusters, and the bark of the branches peels. It is tender.

¶*Rosa rubiginosa,* also called eglantine or sweetbriar rose, is a thorny bush that grows to ten feet high and spreads. The single-petaled flowers are shades of pink and white. It is once-blooming, fragrant, and hardy.

¶*Rosa rugosa* 'Alba' is a bushy, heavily thorned shrub that grows to four feet high, with medium-sized single white flowers. *R. rugosa* 'Rubra' has deep pink flowers. Both have large red to orange hips. Repeat blooming and extremely fragrant, these are among the hardiest of all roses.

¶*Rosa sericea omeiensis pteracantha* is most notable for the large, translucent red thorns that develop on new growth. The shrub, which bears small single-petaled white flowers, grows to approximately ten feet. It has narrow urn-shaped hips in colors of red to orange, is repeat blooming and hardy.

OLD ROSES

Old roses are fascinating to grow as their flowers and growth habits are so different from the modern hybrid teas'. Like the species roses, many of the old roses are more resistant to pests and disease than many modern roses and can also adapt to a wider range of growing conditions than the modern hybrid. Often, they can endure less than perfect care and conditions. Different books and catalogues group the old roses in overlapping categories. For example, a damask rose might also be a shrub. Is it categorized as damask or shrub? In addition, the age of many old roses is obscured by their long breeding and development, even into the twentieth century. The broad dates

below refer to when each was first known, or introduced. Look for old roses primarily through mail-order catalogues, although some specialty nurseries are beginning to carry a small selection of the better-known old roses.

ANCIENT ROSES These are the roses that were known to have been cultivated in ancient times in the eastern and western Mediterranean and in China.

¶Alba roses are hybrids of *R. gallica*, perhaps, and other species roses. They include large shrubby bushes that grow up to seven feet, and some that are prone to climb may reach twenty feet. Their foliage is characteristically blue-green. Once-flowering, the blooms are white or pale pink and are very fragrant and hardy.

¶China roses consist of varieties and hybrids that were cultivated and bred in China. Shrubs growing to four or five feet were first introduced into Europe in 1792. The initial ones introduced were repeat flowering with red or pink blooms. They are tender.

¶Damask roses are varieties of *R. damascena* and are generally shrubby bushes, which grow to seven feet. The summer-damask group is once-flowering, while the autumn damasks flower twice. All are very fragrant and hardy and have flowers of red, pink, or white.

¶Gallica and varieties of *R. gallica* are generally shrubby and grow to four feet high. Hardy, once-flowering, and fragrant, they are deep red, magenta, pink, white, or variegated.

ROSES FROM THE SIXTEENTH AND SEVENTEENTH CENTURIES From this era comes the large, heavy-headed centifolia rose. It is lavishly petaled and very full. ¶Centifolia, also called cabbage rose, rose de Provence, and the Holland rose, is a cross between an alba rose and an autumn damask. Loose shrubs, growing to seven feet, they have blooms in shades of red, pink, or white. They are fragrant and hardy.

ROSES FROM THE EIGHTEENTH CENTURY Of the two roses from this period, one is a mutant and one a cross. ¶Moss roses have buds or canes covered lightly or heavily with furry, sometimes curling "moss." The moss is actually a mutation, a physical change in the makeup of thorns, first known to appear in 1720. Hybrids were developed and introduced from a mossed centifolia starting in the nineteenth century. Generally the moss roses are large bushes growing to six feet or more with flowers pink, white, magenta, or variegated and single petaled or double. The flowers are very fragrant, as is the moss, some are repeat flowering, and all are hardy. New breeding in the twentieth century, primarily of miniatures, has introduced yellow to the color range.

¶Portland roses are probably a cross between an autumn damask and *R. gallica* 'Officinalis'. The colors of the flowers are deep red, magenta, and pink. Smallish shrubs grow to approximately four feet and are repeat blooming and medium hardy.

ROSES FROM THE NINETEENTH CENTURY During this era were bred and cultivated numerous roses, including the first hybrid tea rose. It was eventually to dominate rose breeding and the notion of what defines rose beauty during the twentieth century.

¶Bourbon roses are the result of a cross between an autumn damask and a China rose on what was the Ile de Bourbon, now the Ile de Reunion, an island located in the Indian Ocean off the coast of Madagascar. This was further crossed with gallica and damask hybrids. Colors of the blooms range from reds to pinks and whites and can be variegated. Most are medium-hardy shrubs growing to four or five feet, or are climbers; generally all have fragrant flowers and repeat bloom, often substantial bloom in fall.

¶Hybrid perpetual roses are the result of a cross between a Portland rose and a China hybrid. They are sturdy, repeat flowering, generally scented, and medium-hardy. The colors of the blooms are shades of purple, magenta, pink, or white.

¶Hybrid tea roses are the result of crosses between hybrid perpetuals and tea roses. Since their initial introduction in 1867, there has been much additional breeding with other types of roses to select for color, disease resistance, hardiness, and heat tolerance. Hybrid teas today can be yellow, orange, red, buff, pink, purple, lavender, white, and all shades in between. Their fragrance ranges from nonexistent to notable, and their growth habit is generally a compact bush shape but also includes shrubs and climbers. They have bud-shaped flowers that grow singly rather than in groups, and the flowers, generally large, may be single petaled or be double in varying degrees. Almost all are repeat bloomers, with the newer introductions (often called modern, as described below) the most likely to be so.

¶Noisette roses have as their primary ancestors a hybrid of the species rose *R. moschata* and a China rose. This hybrid was crossed with other roses, especially the teas.

Notable as both shrubs and climbers, noisettes are prolific repeat bloomers and generally scented, excelling in areas with mild-winter climates. Flower colors range from pink, apricot, peach, and buff to crimson. There are also bush types.

¶Tea roses are the result of crosses that occurred well before the nineteenth century in China, though it was not until the nineteenth century that the tea rose was introduced to Europe. Named for their distinctive scent of tea, the repeat-blooming smallish bushes or climbers are loose in form with relatively little foliage, and they thrive in climates with mild winters. The flowers are large, in shades of peach, rose, buff, yellow, and other like hues, and they are very fragrant.

¶Sempervirens ramblers are the result of a cross between *R. sempervirens* and various other roses. A distinctive feature is that they keep their foliage year-round. They bloom once a year, although some have a little repeat bloom in fall. Flowers are small, usually in shades of pink to white, and are fragrant. Numerous canes that grow from the base of the plant make large, weeping shrubs to twelve feet high and more, and the canes readily climb nearby structures.

MODERN ROSES

Modern roses have a huge range of nuanced color, and most have the distinguishing characteristic of repeat bloom throughout the growing season. With the exception of the English roses, most of their blossom forms are pointed and upright, unlike the flattened forms of the old roses. As with the old-rose categories the modern roses tend to be classified confusingly. Some that are listed in different categories possess the same characteristics, and categories that overlap have subcategories as well. Modern roses, particularly the hybrid teas, floribundas, some of the English roses, and miniatures, are readily purchased at nurseries and garden centers. Seek the more unusual modern roses, particularly the shrubs and climbers bred during the first part of the twentieth century, through mail-order sources and specialty nurseries.

¶The English rose (also called new English and the David Austin rose) was first introduced by David Austin, the English plant breeder, in 1961. These exhibit the flat, often cupped and quartered blossom shape and the fragrance of the old roses. Combined with the repeat bloom and the rather compact form of modern roses, they are a cross of old and new.

¶Dwarf polyantha and its climbers bloom in clusters, are repeat flowering, and are medium hardy. Flower shapes and colors vary, and some are single petaled, others double. The shrublike plants are small, and most of the climbers are the result of sports, offshoots of the parent bush but different from the parent.

¶Floribunda and its climbers are roses whose parentage includes hybrid teas and dwarf polyantha roses. Similar to the hybrid tea in many ways, their distinguishing characteristic is masses of flowers in groups along the branches, which may bloom at different times. Colors are myriad and flowers may be single petaled or various forms of double. Their growth is generally shrubby and most are medium hardy.

¶Grandiflora and its climbers are similar to floribundas but larger.

¶Hybrid tea and its climbers are roses that, although introduced in the nineteenth century are considered to have been the first modern rose. The climbers are for the most part sports of the bush rather than bred specifically to climb.

¶Hybrid musks are roses that have a strong fragrance and a shrubby growth pattern, with sizes ranging from three to seven feet. They repeat bloom, especially when well watered and nourished, and are medium hardy. Flowers may be single or double and colors are myriad.

¶Miniature roses were developed from a dwarf China rose that was only five inches high. Most miniatures range from eight inches to eighteen inches. Colors are myriad, and flowers take many forms, both single and double. Growth patterns are generally bushy but vary according to the parentage. Some are climbers as well. Flowers may be single petaled or double, and flat, bud-shaped, or cupped. A group of rosebushes similar to miniatures is called patio roses. These range in size from one and a half feet to three feet.

¶Modern shrub roses almost always include some hybrid tea in their breeding. Their appearance, growth habit, fragrance, and flower shape varies from variety to variety, but generally they are hardy and flower heavily and repeatedly throughout the season of bloom. Size ranges from five to ten feet and the taller ones may be treated as climbers.

¶Multiflora hybrids, which are a type of rambler rose, occurred when the species *R. multiflora* was crossed with other roses. These ramblers almost always have numerous small flowers in large, upward-facing groups. The plant's growth pattern is rather upright. Once-blooming, with occasional repeating in late summer or fall, multiflora ramblers are often fragrant and are medium hardy.

¶Wichuriana hybrids are also types of rambler roses that occurred when the species *R. wichuriana* was crossed with other roses. These ramblers almost always have small flowers that hang in clusters. The plant's growth pattern is loose and spreading. Once-blooming, with occasional repeating in late summer and early fall, these ramblers are generally fragrant and medium hardy.

About growing roses

Roses require ample water, sun, and nutrients to thrive, especially in the early stages of growth. However, some of the old roses and species roses in particular will grow and bloom year after year with little more than rainfall to nourish them and occasional removal of dead wood. In choosing your roses, consider where you will plant them. Roses require a sunny location; as a rule of thumb, consider four hours of full sun the minimum requirement and six hours to be preferable. They can thrive in full sun as well as in partial shade, particularly once they have become well established, after a year or two.

Purchasing a Healthy Rose Plant

Starting with a healthy rose plant is the best insurance for success. It may take years to coddle and shape a plant that starts with poor root and branch structure into the rose you envisioned—time you could spend enjoying your roses.

¶The roots of a healthy rosebush, as in a bare-root rose you can see, should be open and fanning, not twisted and crossing. The branch structure should exhibit strong main branches that do not cross one another. The number of branches recommended varies, but for modern roses such as hybrid teas, grandifloras, and multifloras, three is considered desirable to establish an aesthetic and open framework for the plant.

BARE-ROOT OR POTTED Bare-root roses are dormant. They are without leaves or even tiny hints of buds and look like dry sticks with roots. It is difficult to believe anything will come from these and it takes a leap of faith to buy and plant them, particularly for the first time. Virtually all rosebushes ordered through the mail are shipped bare-root, with the exception of the miniature roses, which are shipped potted.

¶Roses from nurseries and garden centers are sold bare-root in winter and early spring. If you can't plant a bare-root rose when it arrives in the mail, follow the directions on the shipping box about how to store your purchase until you are ready to plant. If you acquired the bare-root rose at a nursery or from another source, keep the roots in water until you can plant. I have kept bare-root roses in a bucket of water for up to two weeks.

¶Any bare-root roses at nurseries that are still unsold at the time dormancy breaks and buds begin to swell are potted, and they are sold this way for the remainder of spring and through summer. Potted roses purchased early in the season either have been held over from the previous year or have been newly potted. In the first instance, the root ball—the combination of soil and roots—will have formed; in the second, it will not have.

¶Planting bare-root roses maximizes success because they are dormant. When the planted bush's dormancy breaks, its growth can proceed with no untoward shocks. Because potted rosebushes are already in the process of growing, transplanting them, whether into the ground or another container, shocks them and disturbs the growing process, and may put the plant at risk.

¶In this book all the instructions are for planting bare-root roses, except in those cases where a rose is most likely to be found only potted. The main difference in the physical aspect of planting roses from containers is the omission of the soil cone over which the bare roots are spread; the root ball of a container-grown rose is placed directly on the potting mix or soil.

To Plant Potted Roses in Containers or in the Ground

Follow directions as for bare-root roses except for these differences. Using clippers, remove any weak, broken, or crossing branches from the bush. Remove any blossoms by cutting at the base of each stem or just above a cluster of five leaves. Submerge the rose and the pot it is in in a bucket of water for an hour or two or up to twenty-four hours before planting.

¶If planting in a container, fill it approximately two-thirds full with potting mix and water thoroughly, until soaked. If planting in the ground, refill the hole approximately two-thirds full with soil.

¶To plant, remove the rosebush from the pot, leaving the ball of roots and soil intact. Place this root ball in the container on top of the potting mixture or soil, positioning the bud union as for bare-root: two inches above the soil line in a mild-winter climate or two inches below in a cold-winter climate. Unlike bare-root roses, potted roses may be fertilized immediately after planting.

¶A potted rose, whether miniature or full size, may be slipped into a decorative cache-pot that is slightly larger than the growing pot. The growing pot must be at least 12 by

24 inches deep. Left in a pot smaller than this, the roots do not have adequate room to grow and develop. Alternatively, a rose in a small pot may be replanted, preferably when dormant, into a larger pot.

HARDINESS AND HEAT Hardiness is determined by the extent of the freezing a rose can tolerate without being killed. Nonhardy or "tender" roses cannot tolerate freezes. Some of the species roses are extremely hardy, while others are quite tender. Hybrid teas and grandiflora roses are generally more tender than the old roses and the modern shrub roses. In cold-winter climate areas, the tender roses need such protection from freezing as coverings of mulch or plastic. The hardiness of roses varies not only from category to category, with one of the hardiest of all roses being the rugosa types that can withstand temperatures to −25 degrees F, but also from variety to variety within the category. Whether purchasing by mail order or at nurseries, check the hardiness of the rose before buying it if you are in a cold-climate area.

¶Conversely, some roses do not tolerate heat well, and in hot climates or areas with hot summers may display weak growth and poor bloom. Check for heat tolerance of each rose in climates that are especially hot.

ORIGINAL OR GRAFTED ROOTS For a number of years hybrid teas have been grafted onto rootstock, even though they may grow perfectly well on their own roots. Grafted roses have a bud union, or graft knot, near the base where the desired rose has been grafted onto rootstock. Grafting is still the norm, but in recent years there has been considerable evidence that roses grown on their own rootstock perform as well if not better than grafted roses. Old and species roses are most commonly grown on their own roots, as are miniature roses. In either instance, the important thing is that the rosebush appear healthy when you receive it. Do note though that often roses on their own rootstock may initially be smaller in size than those that have been grafted.

¶When roses are grafted they are prone to putting forth suckers from the rootstock. These should be cut off at their bases as soon as they appear, as they sap the vigor from the grafted rose.

SOIL, POTTING MIXES, AND PREPARED GROUND

SOIL Soil is a mixture of the three soil particles, sand, silt, and clay, plus any available organic matter. Sand is chemically inactive, so it is the clay and silt and the organic matter that are involved in the complex exchanges of water and plant nutrients. Sand, however, is by far the largest in size of the particles, and the presence of sand means that there will be correspondingly large spaces between soil particles. Sand is responsible for creating an "open" texture in the soil, which allows water movement, including the drainage and porosity necessary for proper soil atmosphere.

¶The organic matter in soils is old plant material, decomposing under constant attack by bacteria and fungi. Over time these organisms liberate mineral elements that are essential to other plants for their growth. Commercial compost is an example of well-decomposed organic matter.

¶An ideal soil would be composed of sand, silt, clay, and organic matter in proportions

that allow good drainage and aeration yet have adequate water- and nutrient-holding capabilities. A good loamy soil is about 60 percent sand, 20 percent silt, and 20 percent clay. Most soils are well under 5 percent organic matter.

POTTING MIXES Commercial potting mixes are much, much higher in organic matter than soil is and much, much lower in sand—more often than not containing no sand. The addition of sand to these mixes greatly improves them, ensuring that roots can reach the water you give them. Vermiculite is considerably lighter than sand and may be used in lieu of it.

PREPARED GROUND Roses grow in all kinds of soil, and may be container grown in potting mixtures, but drainage and ample nutrients are essential for roses to flourish. Consider amending your soil with organic matter to prepare it for planting if it is very sandy, and with organic matter and sand if it is primarily clay. Water that stands or "sheets" on the surface is an indication of compacted soil, which needs organic matter and/or sand.

FERTILIZER

Most commercial fertilizers list their contents as the percentage of each nutrient, in the order nitrogen-phosphorus-potassium, so a 10-10-10 fertilizer would be 10 percent each of nitrogen, phosphorus, and potassium. This is a "balanced" fertilizer, as roses need, containing about equal parts of each major nutrient. As a rule, roses of all kinds will thrive in a home garden setting with applications of a balanced fertilizer specifically for roses. In general, the repeat bloomers such as the hybrid teas and other modern roses require more applications of fertilizer than the single bloomers or the vigorous ramblers and shrubs.

¶Slow-release fertilizers do just that—release their nutrients over time. For container roses use a dilute solution of fish emulsion or a slow-release fertilizer to protect against the possibility of adding too much, which can burn, damage, and even kill the confined plant.

¶There are a number of commercially available fertilizers designed specifically for use on roses from which to choose. Since concentrations vary from manufacturer to manufacturer, follow the instructions on the product you purchase.

PESTS AND DISEASE

Some roses are more susceptible than others to insect damage and disease. The rugosa species roses I grow along my road are never visited by aphids, cucumber beetles, thrips, or mites. Nor are they subject to the three common maladies of mildew, rust, and black spot. 'Double Delight,' which is a beautiful red and white variegated hybrid tea, is covered with aphids as soon as it leafs out. 'Reines des Violettes' is a hybrid perpetual of exceptional beauty that occasionally gets a few black spots but nothing else.  Generally, the old and species roses tend to greater disease resistance and less insect damage than the modern hybrid teas, but with diseases and insect infestations, growing location and climate are also influencing factors. A rose that is perfectly healthy in one location may be subject to disease in another. Keep the plants sheltered from winds, which both damage blooms and foliage and dry out the canes.

¶A healthy rose, regardless of variety, is the best insurance and protection from pests and disease. Above all, roses need water, especially modern roses. Keep them fertilized, and remove spent blooms and any spent foliage. Keep clippings and weeds removed from the area, as these are potential sources of pests and disease. Ensure that there is good air circulation within the branches, particularly in humid locations. If, in spite of all your efforts, a disease or insect infestation appears and threatens your roses, treat them as soon as possible with a commercially available spray or dust designed for rose disease, fungus, or both. Be sure to inquire before purchasing about the content of the sprays and to assess the potential danger from chemicals they may contain. Sprays based on natural substances, such as pyrethrum, are available as well.

¶Mildew presents itself as a whitish powder on the leaves and shoots of the plant. Some roses are quite susceptible to it, others entirely resistant. Black spot appears as black spots on the leaves, which then drop. Rust shows itself in the yellowing and browning of leaves on both the top and undersides.

¶Aphids are the quintessential rose pest. They can entirely cover young shoots and buds and they are quite destructive. They may be washed off with some success, treated with a spray, or smothered with an insecticidal soap or with a mixture of everyday liquid dish soap and water—my preferred method.

¶Other common pests are mites, various caterpillars, and beetles, which chomp circular holes in the leaves.

¶For the diseases and pests prevalent in your area and suggested treatment, consult your local nursery.

PRUNING

Much ado is made about pruning, to the point that growing roses sometimes seems an impossibility for anyone not versed in deep technical knowledge of the craft. However, pruning in its most straightforward form may be thought of as simply shaping the bush by removing unwanted or unnecessary growth, generally with small pruning clippers or, for mature woody plants, with pruning shears. When you cut even a stem, you are pruning the bush. Pruning increases the strength and vigor of the wanted growth. "Hard pruning" means cutting the existing growth back by as much as one-half. This is useful when a bush is weak, as it forces needed vigor in the plant. Also, hard pruning is considered responsible for larger blooms.

¶Pruning of repeat-blooming roses in mild-winter climates may be done in late winter or early spring, when the plants are dormant or as dormant as they are going to become. In areas with cold-winter climates pruning should be done in spring when there is no longer any danger of freezes, as once pruned the rosebush is more vulnerable to freeze damage. With single-bloomers in any climate, any pruning needed should be done in summer after the bloom is over.

¶Some roses need more attention to pruning than others to bloom well and to look their best. Hybrid tea roses are an example. An unpruned hybrid tea will bloom, but the plant will look scraggly and the blooms will tend to be smaller than they should be, and sparse. Many modern ramblers and shrub roses as well as old roses are among those that require little pruning other than the removal of dead wood to look gorgeous and to produce profusions of blooms. Some old-rose experts recommend leaving old roses unpruned for three years in order to ascertain the natural shape of the bush, and then pruning according to its shape and growth pattern. Species roses require only the periodic removal of dead wood and shearing, if desired, to control size somewhat.

¶The width of roses, in addition to their height, is a significant factor in their appearance, but no special techniques are needed in pruning width. As a rule of thumb, follow the growth pattern of the rosebush rather than imposing your own. This is particularly applicable to the older roses.

¶For potted roses another part of the shaping process is the size of the pot, since restricting the roots restricts the top growth. Roses can be kept in a minimum-size pot of 12 by 24 inches indefinitely, but repotting to 24 by 38 inches after several years is recommended for a large bush, or even starting in a large, fifteen-gallon-size container. Imagine the larger container, with its extra room for the roots to grow and spread. These thriving roots have an enhanced capacity to deliver extra nutrients to the bush above, allowing it to further grow and spread.

¶It is actually quite fun to stand back, looking at a rosebush, and with the eye of an artist or a surgeon to decide where to apply the snip of the pruning clippers that season. Remember, a rose grows for years and years, and no clip is really final, just a step in an ongoing process.

¶Rather than give instructions here on the pruning methods and styles for all the rose categories, each entry on a rose gives the pruning specifics for that plant. These instructions may be applied to other rosebushes of the same category.

Container Roses For Windowsills Or Fire Escapes

The enchanting forms, colors, and foliage of miniature or other small roses are often lost in a garden setting, but they are highlighted when the diminutive roses are container-grown in small spaces, such as windowsills, windowboxes, and fire escapes. Small plantings can even be kept temporarily on a tabletop, where their charms can be admired close at hand. ❧ It was not until I saw a display of miniatures at a local rose show that I realized how truly varied and distinct each is, with characteristics and colors as fascinating as their larger counterparts'. Cupped old-fashioned-type blossoms adorn some, while the perfect pointed buds of the hybrid tea adorn others. Roses other than miniatures that are particularly suitable for windowboxes or for container planting on fire escapes or small balconies are some of the dwarf polyanthas and any other type bred small. Check labels to gauge which will demand no more space than you can provide. ❧ Roses of any size or type that grow outdoors become dormant in winter. They should be pruned then, during early winter in mild climates and during early spring in climates with cold winters. Rosebushes grown inside on windowsills require, over winter, an outdoor location or an artificial situation where they too can become dormant. Dormancy may be forced by removing most of the leaves from the bush, gently taking the bush from its container and brushing away the soil, and storing the rosebush, wrapped in paper or ventilated plastic, in the refrigerator for one and a half to two months.

ROSES IN CACHE-POTS

A quick and effortless way of enjoying an indoor windowsill of blooming roses is to buy potted bushes with buds just starting to open and display them slipped into cache-pots. With water and sun the rosebushes will provide a seasonful of blooms that can be clipped and made into tiny bouquets, worn in pin-on bud vases, or used sugared or fresh to garnish and decorate cakes, ice creams, and other confections. ¶ Choose the colors of roses and cache-pots that suit your fancy, and then when the blooming season ends, come fall, cut back the trusses of roses, and put the potted bushes in a cool place for the winter. ¶ **HOW TO DO IT** ¶ Choose a windowsill with at least four hours of full sun. For each 6-inch potted rosebush, choose a cache-pot just large enough to hold the plant. Place a few pieces of gravel, small rocks, or bits of broken pottery on the bottom of the cache-pot. Submerge the rosebushes, still in their original pots, in buckets of water for an hour or two to saturate the potting mix. Slip each pot into a cache-pot. ¶ Fertilize when planting and every three or four weeks thereafter during the season of bloom, with a weak solution of fish emulsion or other liquid fertilizer. Keep potting mix moist to the touch. Once every three or four months, water daily for three days to leach out accumulated salts, fertilizing afterward. ¶ During the season of bloom cut away any exceptionally thick or large branches and leggy growth, and keep spent blooms removed. To initiate a dormant period, remove most of the leaves and any blooms that continue to appear in fall and early winter. Put the potted rose outside in a mild-winter climate or in a garage or other protected indoor location in a cold-winter climate for at least one month and as long as three months, or the equivalent of winter in your area. Water as needed to prevent the potting mixture from drying out. Return the container to the indoor windowsill, and when new buds begin to swell, cut back every branch to reduce the size of the plant by one-third.

Hybrid miniature rose
Various colors
18 to 24 inches high
Fragrance: medium
Bloom: repeated

❧

What You Need
5 potted miniature rosebushes,
6-inch pot size
Location with at least 4 hours full sun
5 cache-pots just large enough
to hold the rosebushes
Gravel, small rocks, or bits of
broken pottery
Small pruning clippers
Slow-release rose fertilizer
or liquid fertilizer

❧

When to Buy
Potted rosebushes (only), early spring
from mail-order catalogues, spring
through late fall from nurseries

❧

When to Plant
Potted rosebushes (only),
spring through fall

❧

Miniature moss roses

The most striking feature of a moss rose, whether full size or miniature, is the soft, furry, mosslike texture of the stems, leaves, and buds. Moss roses, which have the old-fashioned cup-shaped blossoms, were quite popular during the age of old roses, before the time of the modern hybrid teas. Since then little breeding of them has been done, except among the miniature roses. With its heavily mossed buds and stems, sharp thorns, and cupping flowers, pale pink 'Dresden Doll' has all the attributes of the old, full-sized moss roses, but it blooms repeatedly. ¶ **HOW TO DO IT** ¶ Choose a location with at least four hours of full sun. For five rosebushes, choose a windowbox or other container at least 24 inches long, 12 inches wide, and 18 inches deep. Cover the bottom with a layer of gravel, small rocks, or bits of broken pottery. Make a mixture of two-thirds potting mix and one-third sand. Fill the container approximately one-half full with the mixture and water thoroughly, until soaked. ¶ Use pruning clippers to cut back any broken or bruised branches, and remove fully bloomed flowers. Submerge the rosebushes, still in their original pots, in buckets of water for an hour or two or as long as twenty-four hours, before planting. ¶ To plant, remove each rosebush from its pot. Leave the ball of roots and soil intact. Place this root ball in the container on top of the potting mixture, and position the rosebush so that the topmost roots can be situated 2 inches below the soil line. ¶ Fill in with the remaining mixture, constantly tamping it firmly around the root ball. Water gently until the potting mixture is saturated and has settled, adding more mixture if necessary. Fertilize at the time of planting and then every three to four weeks. ✍

'Dresden Doll'
Miniature moss rose
Light pink
16 to 20 inches high
Fragrance: slight
Bloom: repeated
❧

What You Need
5 potted 'Dresden Doll' rosebushes
Location with at least 4 hours full sun
1 windowbox or other container at least
24 inches long, 12 inches wide,
and 18 inches deep
Gravel, small rocks, or bits of
broken pottery
Potting mix
Sand
Small pruning clippers
Slow-release rose fertilizer
or liquid fertilizer
❧

When to Buy
Potted rosebushes (only), spring through
fall from mail-order catalogues
and specialty nurseries
❧

When to Plant
Potted rosebushes (only),
spring through fall
❧

Keep well watered thereafter, maintaining moisture in the root zone. ¶ During the season of bloom, cut away any exceptionally thick or large branches and leggy growth, and keep spent blooms removed to help maintain the miniature size and shape. In late winter or early spring, when the rosebushes are dormant and the buds have just begun to swell, cut back every branch to reduce plant size by one-third.

Tiny rose trees

Tiny rose standards, when their rounded heads are in full bloom, recall for me illustrations of *Alice in Wonderland when she popped into the rose garden, surrounded by bushes of big, round rose blooms each with a face.* ¶ *Tree roses, or standards, are created by budding a rose type to a bare rootstock trunk at a certain height. Miniatures are generally budded to a trunk twelve to eighteen inches above the soil level. The budded upper part is clipped and maintained in a round shape.* ¶ *Rose standards may be purchased already shaped. The gardener has only to plant the tree, and then as it grows and blooms during summer and fall, judiciously clip straggling growth to maintain the roundness. In late winter or early spring, more severe pruning gives the new growth an even start.* ¶ **HOW TO DO IT** ¶ Choose a location with at least four hours of full sun. For five rosebushes, choose five containers each at least 8 inches in diameter and 10 inches deep with a hole in the bottom. Cover the bottom with a layer of gravel, small rocks, or bits of broken pottery. Make a mixture of two-thirds potting mix and one-third sand. Fill the container approximately one-half full with the mixture and water thoroughly, until soaked. ¶ Use pruning clippers to cut back any broken or bruised branches, and remove fully bloomed flowers. Submerge the rosebushes, still in their original pots, in buckets of water for an hour or two or as long as twenty-four hours, before planting. ¶ To plant, remove the rosebushes from their pots. Leave the ball of roots and soil intact. Place this root ball in the container on top of the potting mixture, and position the rosebush so that the beginning of the roots can be situated 2 inches below the soil line. ¶ Fill in with the remaining mixture, constantly tamping it firmly around the root ball. Water gently until the potting mixture is saturated and has settled, adding more mixture if necessary. Fertilize at the time of planting and then every three to four weeks. Keep well watered thereafter, main- 🖅

'Galaxy', red
'Snow Twinkle', white
Hybrid miniature rose tree
12 to 18 inches high
Fragrance: slight
Bloom: repeated
❧

What You Need
3 potted 'Galaxy' and 2 'Snow Twinkle'
or other hybrid miniature rose trees
Location with at least 4 hours full sun
5 containers, each at least 8 inches in
diameter and 10 inches deep with
a hole in the bottom
Gravel, small rocks, or bits
of broken pottery
Potting mix
Sand
Small pruning clippers
Slow-release rose fertilizer
or liquid fertilizer
❧

When to Buy
Potted rosebushes (only), spring through
fall from mail-order catalogues
and specialty nurseries
❧

When to Plant
Potted rosebushes (only),
spring through fall
❧

taining moisture at the root zone at all times during the period of growth and bloom. Once every three or four months, water daily for three days to leach out accumulated salts, fertilizing afterward. ¶ During the season of bloom, cut away any exceptionally thick or large branches and leggy growth and keep spent blooms removed, to help maintain miniature size and shape. To initiate a dormant period, remove most of the leaves and any blooms that continue to appear in fall and early winter. Put the container outside or in a garage or other cold indoor location for at least one month and as long as three months, or the equivalent of winter in your area. Water as needed to prevent the potting mixture from drying out. Bring the container back to its window indoors, and when new buds begin to swell cut back branches to reduce plant size by one-third.

Potted 'Margot Koster'

Although I have heard that orange-hued modern roses generally have fallen into disfavor, the delicate rose-salmon shade of 'Margo Koster' must be an exception. It is a splendid rose for planting in containers because of its small size, hardiness, full and prolific bloom, lush bright green foliage, and the fact that pruning consists primarily of removing dead flowers and cutting away old or dead growth. Since this rose is also among the few of the dwarf polyantha group that are noticeably scented, it is tempting to grow, particularly for the gardener with limited space. **¶ HOW TO DO IT ¶** Choose a location with at least four hours of full sun. Choose a container at least 18 inches in diameter and at least 24 inches deep. Cover the bottom with a layer of gravel, small rocks, or bits of broken pottery. Make a mixture of two-thirds potting mix and one-third sand. Fill the container approximately one-half full with the mixture and water thoroughly, until soaked. ¶ Use pruning clippers to cut off any broken or bruised roots ½ inch above the break or bruise. Cut back each branch by one-third, cutting about ¼ inch above an outward-facing bud. Remove any weak, broken, or crossing branches. Submerge the roots in a bucket of water for an hour or two or as long as twenty-four hours, before planting. ¶ To plant, add some of the remaining soil mixture to the container, mounding it in the shape of a cone. The cone should be sufficiently tall that the rosebush, when set upon it, can have the roots well covered with soil and the bud union, if there is one, can be situated 2 inches above the soil line if planting in a mild-winter climate or 2 inches below in a cold-winter climate. When you place the rosebush on the cone, fan the roots over the cone's surface. Holding the rose in position, fill the container with potting mixture, constantly tamping the mix firmly around the roots. ✏

'Margo Koster'
Dwarf polyantha rose
Rose-salmon to orange
18 to 24 inches high
Fragrance: medium
Bloom: repeated

❧

What You Need
1 bare-root 'Margo Koster' rosebush
Location with at least 4 hours full sun
1 container at least 18 inches
in diameter and 24 inches deep
Gravel, small rocks, or bits
of broken pottery
Potting mix
Sand
Small pruning clippers
Slow-release rose fertilizer
or liquid fertilizer

❧

When to Buy
Bare-root, winter or early spring from
mail-order catalogues and specialty
nurseries (potted, spring through
summer from specialty nurseries)

❧

When to Plant
Bare-root, late winter or early spring
(potted, spring through summer)

❧

Water gently until the potting mixture is saturated and has settled, adding more mixture if necessary. Keep well watered thereafter, maintaining moist potting mix. ¶ Fertilize after the bush has leafed out and every three or four weeks thereafter with a slow-release fertilizer, or every month with a weak solution of a liquid fertilizer such as fish emulsion. Once every three or four months, water daily for three days to leach out accumulated salts, fertilizing afterward. ¶ In late winter or early spring, when the rosebush is dormant and the buds have just begun to swell, prune by removing any twiggy or dead wood.

Container

roses for

balconies

and patios

*S*ince almost any rose can be successfully grown in a container, choice becomes dictated by personal preference and the constraints of the environment. With a large patio or terrace  one might even plant a hardy pillar rose, such as a 'Sally Holmes'. Large spaces are amenable to tall rose trees, too, but on a small balcony a midsize tree or a shrubby patio rose would be a better choice. ❧ Containers of roses can be moved from one location to another, making a changing display possible, and as a rosarian friend recently told me, not only does she not have to dig those deep holes, she has also annexed more room to plant in. Such are the virtues of growing roses in containers that now not only are her yards full of roses, so are her steps, porch, patio, and any other stand where she can fit a container. ❧ Little additional care is necessary for container-grown roses, other than giving them a thorough and steady extra watering every three or four months to leach out any accumulated salts, and using a slow-release fertilizer in order to avoid the risk of overfertilizing and burning the plants, since they are in a confined environment. Repotting after two or three years may be desirable if the original container was not adequate for the eventual root growth. Larger roses generally have a larger root system than smaller roses, and this is a consideration when choosing roses for particular containers and their locations.

Rugosa cache-pot

Rosebushes kept in plain containers or planters make an instant and elegant display when placed in cache-pots or even baskets. By choosing hardy, tough roses that are relatively immune to freezes, insect damage, and disease, and which demand no pruning other than a yearly clipping, one can maintain a striking garden with minimum upkeep. ¶ The rugosa roses and their hybrids fit the description above, also have a wonderful fragrance, and they bloom repeatedly. Their hips are among the most beautiful in rosedom, plump and rounded. ¶ **HOW TO DO IT** ¶ Choose a location with at least four hours of full sun. Choose a container at least 18 inches in diameter and at least 24 inches deep. Cover the bottom with a layer of gravel, small rocks, or bits of broken pottery. Make a mixture of two-thirds potting mix and one-third sand. Fill the container approximately one-half full with part of the mixture and water thoroughly, until soaked. ¶ Use pruning clippers to cut back any broken or bruised roots $1/2$ inch above the break or bruise. Cut each branch back by one-third, cutting about $1/4$ inch above an outward-facing bud. Remove any weak, broken, or crossing branches. Submerge the roots in a bucket of water for an hour or two or as long as twenty-four, before planting. ¶ To plant, add some of the remaining soil mixture to the container, mounding it in the shape of a cone. The cone should be sufficiently tall that the rosebush, when set upon it, can have the roots well covered with soil and the bud union, if there is one, can be situated 2 inches above the soil line if planted in a mild-winter climate or 2 inches below in a cold-winter climate. When you place the rosebush on the cone, fan the roots over the cone's surface. Holding the rose in position, fill the container with potting mixture, constantly tamping it firmly around the roots. Water gently until the potting mixture is saturated and has ✒

'Hansa'
Rugosa hybrid rose
3 to 4 feet high
Pink
Fragrance: intense
Bloom: repeated

❧

What You Need
1 bare-root 'Hansa' rosebush
Location with at least 4 hours full sun
Terra-cotta jar or other container
at least 18 inches in diameter
and 24 inches deep
Gravel, small rocks, or bits of
broken pottery
Potting mix
Sand
Small pruning clippers
Slow-release rose fertilizer
or liquid fertilizer

❧

When to Buy
Bare-root, winter or early spring from
mail-order catalogues and specialty
nurseries (potted, spring through
summer from specialty nurseries)

❧

When to Plant
Bare-root, late winter or early spring
(potted, spring through summer)

❧

settled, adding more mixture if necessary. Keep well watered thereafter, maintaining moist potting mix during the season of growth and bloom. ¶ Fertilize after leaves have appeared and every three to four weeks afterward, with a slow-release rose fertilizer or a liquid fertilizer, such as fish emulsion. Stop fertilizing in approximately early September in areas with mild-winter climates, late July in areas with cold winter climates. Begin fertilizing again when the bushes begin to emerge from dormancy. Once every three or four months, water daily for three days to leach out accumulated salts, fertilizing afterward. ¶ If desired in late winter or early spring, when the rosebush is dormant and the buds have just begun to swell, use hedge clippers or pruning shears to shear back the bush by one-half or the desired amount, and remove any dead wood.

WHITE ROSE COLLECTION

Containers planted with different varieties of white roses reflect the brilliance of the moon and seem to diffuse its white light. Whether you're outside at night to eat with friends around a candlelit table or for solitary stargazing, the white roses provide a soft gleam at the edges of the dark. ¶ Daylight shows off the sophistication of the monochromatic palette and the variation of shape and size in the blooms and their foliage. Some, like 'Iceberg,' are the white of a breaking wave's froth, others the color of thick cream or of snow under a spring sun. A mixture of single-petaled varieties, full and heavily petaled types, and classics such as 'Fran Druski' make for interest as does a combination of blue-green, apple green, and forest green foliage. ¶ **HOW TO DO IT** ¶ Choose a location with at least four hours of full sun. Choose containers at least 18 inches in diameter and at least 24 inches deep, some larger for visual variety. Cover the bottoms with a layer of gravel, small rocks, or bits of broken pottery. Make a mixture of two-thirds potting mix and one-third sand. Fill the containers approximately one-half full with the mixture and water thoroughly, until soaked. ¶ Use pruning clippers to cut off any broken or bruised roots $\frac{1}{2}$ inch above the break or bruise. Cut back each branch by one-third, to $\frac{1}{4}$ inch above an outward-facing bud. Submerge the roots in a bucket of water for an hour or two or as long as twenty-four hours, before planting. ¶ To plant, add some of the remaining soil mixture to the containers, mounding it in the shape of a cone. Each cone should be sufficiently tall that the rosebush, when set upon it, can have the roots well covered with soil and the bud union, if there is one, can be situated 2 inches above the soil line if planting in a mild-winter climate or 2 inches below in a cold-winter climate. When you place each rosebush in turn on its cone, fan the roots over the cone's surface. Holding the rose in position, fill in the container with potting mixture, constantly tamping the mix firmly ✒

'Iceberg'
Floribunda rose
White
3 feet high
Fragrance: medium
Bloom: repeated

❧

What You Need
5 'Iceberg' rosebushes or a
mixture of white roses
Location with at least 4 hours full sun
5 containers at least 18 inches across
and 24 inches deep,
some larger than others
Gravel, small rocks, or bits
of broken pottery
Potting mix
Sand
Small pruning clippers
Slow-release rose fertilizer
or liquid fertilizer

❧

When to Buy
Bare-root, winter through spring from
specialty nurseries and mail-order
catalogues (potted, spring through summer
from specialty nurseries)

❧

When to Plant
Bare-root, winter through early spring
(potted, spring through summer)

❧

around the roots. ¶ Water gently until the potting mixture is saturated and has settled, adding more mixture if necessary. Keep well watered thereafter to maintain moisture in the root zone during the period of growth and bloom. ¶ Fertilize after the bushes have leafed out, and then every three or four weeks with a slow-release rose fertilizer, or with a weak solution of a liquid fertilizer such as fish emulsion. Once every three or four months, water daily for three days to leach out accumulated salts, fertilizing afterward. ¶ In late winter or early spring, when the rosebushes are dormant and the buds have just begun to swell, prune. Remove any dead wood and weak or crossing branches. Cut the branches back by one-third, making each cut about $1/4$ inch above an outward-facing bud.

A classic old rose

Named for the famous gardens at Malmaison that were created for the Empress Josephine, Napoleon's first wife, 'Souvenir de la Malmaison' was introduced in 1843, thirty years after Josephine was set aside in favor of Marie Louise. Its large, pale flesh-pink, double flowers are cupped and quartered and have a strong fragrance that wafts on the air from spring through fall, as this rose blooms repeatedly. ¶ It is the epitome of the old roses. Growing it in a container showcases its exceptional blossoms and makes it readily accessible for cut flowers to bring inside. ¶ **HOW TO DO IT** ¶ Choose a location with at least four hours of full sun. Choose a container at least 18 inches in diameter and at least 24 inches deep. Cover the bottom with a layer of gravel, small rocks, or bits of broken pottery. Make a mixture of two-thirds potting mix and one-third sand. Fill the container approximately one-half full with part of the mixture and water thoroughly, until soaked. ¶ Use pruning clippers to cut off any broken or bruised roots ½ inch above the break or bruise. Cut each branch back by one-third, cutting about ¼ inch above an outward-facing bud. Remove any weak, broken, or crossing branches. ¶ Add some of the remaining soil mixture to the container, mounding it in the shape of a cone. The cone should be sufficiently tall that the rosebush, when set upon it, can have the roots well covered with soil and the bud union, if there is one, can be situated 2 inches above the soil line if planted in a mild-winter climate and 2 inches below in a cold-winter climate. When you place the rosebush on the cone fan the roots over the cone's surface. Holding the rose in position, fill the container with potting mixture, constantly tamping it firmly around the roots. ¶ Water gently until the potting mixture is saturated and has settled, adding more mixture if necessary. Keep well watered thereafter, maintaining moist soil. ¶ Fertilize after leaves have appeared and every three to four weeks afterward, with a ✒

'Souvenir de la Malmaison'
Bourbon rose
Pale, cream flesh-pink
turning white
3 to 4 feet high
Fragrance: intense
Bloom: repeated
❧

What You Need
1 bare-root 'Souvenir de
la Malmaison' rosebush
Location with at least 4 hours full sun
1 container at least 18 inches
in diameter and 24 inches deep
Gravel, small rocks, or bits
of broken pottery
Potting mix
Sand
Small pruning clippers
Slow-release rose fertilizer
or liquid fertilizer
❧

When to Buy
Bare-root, winter or early spring
from mail-order catalogues and specialty
nurseries (potted, spring through summer
from specialty nurseries)
❧

When to Plant
Bare-root, in late winter or early spring
(potted, spring through summer)
❧

slow-release rose fertilizer or a weak solution of a liquid fertilizer, such as fish emulsion. Stop fertilizing in approximately early September in areas with mild-winter climates, late July in areas with cold-winter climates. Begin fertilizing again when the bushes begin to emerge from dormancy. Once every three or four months, water daily for three days to leach out accumulated salts, fertilizing afterward. ¶ Remove blooms as they fade, cutting each at the base of a stem or just above a cluster of at least five leaves. In late winter or early spring, when the rosebushes are dormant and the buds have just begun to swell, prune the bushes by removing twiggy growth. Thin out dead or woody canes at the bottom, and cut back the remaining canes by one-quarter to one-third. Cut back the lateral branches to about 6 inches long, as it is on the new laterals that flowering growth will appear.

A pillar of 'Sally Holmes'

The huge single-petal blossoms of 'Sally Holmes' in clusters of twenty-five or more blooms are so tightly packed and abundant that from a distance you think you are looking at a pink and white rhododendron or hydrangea in full flush, instead of a rosebush. ¶ Although it is a large shrub rose, it is adaptable to being container grown, and when given a large container and the support of a tripod or cone it becomes a magnificent pillar of bloom. Tripods or cones, fashioned after those in French and English gardens to support pillar roses, can be purchased through specialty garden shops or nurseries or made from heavy-gauge wire. The rose's height and size can be regulated by pruning. ¶ **HOW TO DO IT** ¶ Choose a location with at least four hours of full sun. Choose a container at least 24 inches in diameter and at least 36 inches deep. Cover the bottom with a layer of gravel, small rocks, or bits of broken pottery. Make a mixture of two-thirds potting mix and one-third sand, or use a purchased mixture that is one-third sand. Fill the container approximately one-third full with part of the mixture and water thoroughly, until soaked. ¶ Use pruning clippers to cut off any broken or bruised roots 1/2 inch above the break or bruise. Cut away any weak, broken, or crossing branches. Cut each branch back by one-third, cutting about 1/4 inch above an outward-facing bud. ¶ Submerge the roots of the bare-root rose in a bucket of water for an hour or two or as long as twenty-four hours before planting. ¶ To plant, add some of the remaining soil mixture to the container, mounding it in the shape of a cone. The cone should be sufficiently tall that the roots, when set upon it, can be well covered with soil. When you place the rosebush on the cone, fan the roots over the cone's surface. Holding the rosebush in position, fill the container with the potting mixture, constantly tamping it firmly around the roots so that the bud union of the trunk and the rootstock, if there is ⚡

'Sally Holmes'
Modern shrub rose
Soft pink turning to white
5 to 10 feet high
Fragrance: slight
Bloom: repeated

❧

What You Need
1 bare-root 'Sally Holmes' rosebush
Location with at least 4 hours full sun
1 container at least 24 inches
in diameter and 36 inches deep
Gravel, small rocks, or bits
of broken pottery
Potting mix
Sand
Small pruning clippers
6-foot rose tripod or cone
Slow-release rose fertilizer
or liquid fertilizer

❧

When to Buy
Bare-root, winter or early spring from
mail-order catalogues and specialty
nurseries (potted, spring through summer
from specialty nurseries)

❧

When to Plant
Bare-root, late winter or early spring
(potted, spring through summer)

❧

one, will be 2 inches above the soil line if planted in a mild-winter climate, or 2 inches below in a cold-winter climate. ¶ Water gently until the potting mixture is saturated and has settled, adding more mix if necessary. Keep well watered thereafter, maintaining moist potting mix during the period of growth and bloom. Position the tripod or cone in the container, pushing it $1\frac{1}{2}$ to 2 feet deep. As the rose canes grow, weave or tie them to the tripod. ¶ Fertilize after leaves have appeared and every three to four weeks afterward, with a slow-release rose fertilizer or a liquid fertilizer such as fish emulsion. Stop fertilizing in approximately early September in areas with mild-winter climates, late July in areas with cold-winter climates. Begin fertilizing again when the bushes begin to emerge from dormancy. Once every three or four months, water daily for three days to leach out accumulated salts, fertilizing afterward.

ROSES FOR

SMALL

GARDEN

SPACES

Many a magnificent rambling rose or other climber needs only a square foot or two of ground space as long as it has room to go up. I have long been astounded by the roses that grow up stone walls of French village houses from no more than a square foot of earth, on the edges of cobbled roads where cars and trucks rumble by within a hand's reach of the rose canes. ❧ Even if you have only a small garden space, the array of roses you can grow successfully is huge, with many shapes, colors, and forms from which to choose that include climbers and ramblers, both old and modern ❧ Among the modern roses are those bred specifically for small spaces, such as the patio rose. The medium-sized modern landscape or ground-cover roses, as they are sometimes called, require minimal care. A number of the smaller hybrid teas fit nicely into a limited garden space as well. Do consider that growing roses in a constrained space, whether climbers or bushes, may require fastidious pruning to keep them from taking over or dominating your garden. The rewards of having a rose you love in your garden will no doubt compensate the effort.

A violet rambler

On a visit to a small rose nursery on California's Mendocino coast, I saw this rose entwined in a pine tree, from whence it draped and rambled across an old-fashioned trellis. The effect was one of a mass of blended colors, shocking deep violet tones with brilliant purples, rose-mauve, lavender blues, and pearl grays. I immediately said "I'll take one." They were sold out for that year, but the next year I ordered early. ¶ A rambler in the grand style, it can nevertheless be grown in a small ground area, if you have room for it to climb over a fence, or up a wall. ¶ **HOW TO DO IT** ¶ Choose a location against a wall or a fence with at least four hours of sun. Dig a hole approximately 1½ feet across, 1½ feet deep, and 1 to 1½ feet out from the structure. Buy a trellis or build a simple one as follows. Attach three or four lengths of strong wire to a sturdy stake driven into the ground behind the planting hole and attach the loose ends of the wire firmly to the eaves of the roof or to the fence. Use pruning clippers to trim the rosebush, cutting off any broken or bruised roots ½ inch above the break or bruise. Cut away broken or crossing branches but do not cut back other branches' tips. Submerge the roots of the rosebush in a bucket of water for an hour or two or as long as twenty-four hours, before you plant it. ¶ Refill the hole with some of the loose soil, mounding it in the shape of a cone. The cone should be sufficiently tall that the rosebush, when set upon it, can have the roots well covered with soil and the bud union, if there is one, can be situated 2 inches above the soil line if planted in a mild-winter climate, or 2 inches below in a cold-winter climate. When you place the rosebush on the cone, fan the roots over the cone's surface. Holding the rose in position, fill in the hole with the soil, constantly tamping it firmly around the roots. Start a hose trickling at the edge of ✒

'Vielchenblau'
Multiflora rambling rose
Violet-blue
12 to 15 feet high
Fragrance: medium
Bloom: spring; repeated late summer in
areas with mild winters
❧

What You Need
1 bare-root 'Vielchenblau' rosebush
3 square feet of prepared ground with
at least 4 hours full sun
Small pruning clippers
Wall or fence
Purchased trellis or wire and stake
Balanced rose fertilizer
Gardener's tape
❧

When to Buy
Bare-root, winter or early spring from
mail-order catalogues or specialty nurseries
(potted, spring through summer from
specialty nurseries)
❧

When to Plant
Bare-root (only), late winter or early
spring (potted, spring through summer)
❧

the hole and continue to let it run until the soil is saturated and has settled, adding more soil if necessary. ¶ Water regularly thereafter during the season of growth and bloom, to ensure adequate water at the root zone. Fertilize after leaves have appeared and every three to four weeks afterward, with a balanced rose fertilizer. Stop fertilizing in approximately early September in areas with mild-winter climates, late July in areas with cold-winter climates. Begin fertilizing again when the bushes begin to emerge from dormancy. ¶ To train the rose to climb the wall or fence or a trellis, tie the canes to the wires with gardener's tape or weave the trellis. ¶ Prune when flowering is finished in summer. Cut branches back by about one-third and remove any remaining flowers, as well as any dead or woody growth.

'MERMAID' CLIMBING AN ADOBE WALL

The first 'Mermaid' rose I saw had scaled the gated and roofed wall that surrounded the interior courtyard of a California hillside adobe house. Massed with butter yellow single-petal blooms set off by glossy dark green foliage, it had risen more than thirty feet, spilled onto and crossed the shingle roof, and then encircled a bell set in an alcove of the wall. ¶ From late spring through fall, 'Mermaid' blooms continuously. It is virtually free of pests and diseases, and unless it becomes too rampant, it needs no pruning, other than to cut away dead wood at the end of its blooming season. ¶ **HOW TO DO IT** ¶ Choose a location against a wall, with at least four hours of sun and facing south if possible. Dig a hole approximately 1½ feet across, 1½ feet deep, and 1 to 1½ feet out from the wall. ¶ Buy a trellis or build a simple one as follows. Attach three or four lengths of strong wire to a sturdy stake driven into the ground behind where the rose will be planted and attach the loose ends of the wire firmly at the top, preferably to the eaves of a roof. Use pruning clippers to cut off any broken or bruised roots ½ inch above the break or bruise. Cut back each branch by one third to ¼ inch above an outward-facing bud. Cut away any crossing branches. Submerge the roots in a bucket of water for an hour or two or as long as twenty-four hours before planting. ¶ To plant, refill the hole with some of the loose soil, mounding it in the shape of a cone. The cone should be sufficiently tall that the rosebush, when set upon it, can have the roots be well covered with soil and the bud union, if there is one, can be situated 2 inches above the soil line if planted in a mild-winter climate, or 2 inches below in a cold-winter climate. When you place the rosebush on the cone, fan the roots over the cone's surface. Holding the rose in position, fill in the hole with the soil, constantly tamping it ✒

'Mermaid'
Rosa bracteata *hybrid*
climbing rose
Yellow
20 to 30 feet high
Fragrance: medium
Bloom: repeated

❧

What You Need
1 bare-root 'Mermaid' rosebush
3 square feet of prepared ground with
at least 4 hours full sun
Small pruning clippers
Wire and stake or purchased trellis
Balanced rose fertilizer
Gardener's tape

❧

When to Buy
Bare-root, winter or early spring from
mail-order catalogues or specialty nurseries
(potted, spring through summer from
specialty nurseries)

❧

When to Plant
Bare-root, late winter or early spring
(potted, spring through summer)

❧

firmly around the roots. ¶ Start a hose trickling at the edge of the hole and continue to let it run until the soil is saturated and has settled, adding more soil if necessary. Keep the bush well watered, maintaining a moist root zone during the season of growth and bloom. Fertilize after leaves have appeared and every three to four weeks afterward, with a balanced rose fertilizer. Stop fertilizing in approximately early September in areas with mild-winter climates, late July in areas with cold-winter climates. Begin fertilizing again when bushes begin to emerge from dormancy. To train the rose onto a wall or trellis, gently tie the canes with gardener's tape to the wires or trellis. ¶ To prune, cut away dead wood at end of the blooming season. In late winter or early spring, when the bush is dormant and the buds have just begun to swell, cut back or cut off branches to shape.

An arranger's garden rose

*J*ust Joey' has numerous qualities to recommend *it, not only for a small garden but for any garden. Its buds are deep rose-apricot, unfolding to amber, and finally when full blown the rose's shade is softest blushed apricot. The flowers are large but not blowsy and in a vase hold for several days even in full bloom. The rosebush itself is tidy and able to produce its abundant crop of fragrant flowers on a bush three feet high and only two feet wide. The early spring foliage is a deep, rich mahogany that turns dark green in summer and tones of bronze in fall. ¶ 'Just Joey' blooms from spring through fall without falling victim to disease or pests. This along with its appearance and fragrance makes it a garden rose favored by commercial growers, who cut and ship it for the flower market seven months or more of the year.*

¶ **HOW TO DO IT** ¶ Choose a location with at least four hours of full sun. Dig a hole approximately 1½ feet across and 1½ feet deep. Use the pruning clippers to cut off any broken or bruised roots ½ inch above the break or bruise. Cut away any weak, broken, or crossing branches. Cut back each branch by one-third, to ¼ inch above an outward-facing bud. Submerge the roots in a bucket of water for an hour or two or as long as twenty-four hours, before planting. ¶ To plant, refill the hole with some of the loose soil, mounding it in the shape of a cone. The cone should be sufficiently tall that the rosebush, when set upon it, can have the roots be well covered with soil and the bud union, if there is one, can be situated 2 inches above the soil line if planted in a mild-winter climate or 2 inches below in a cold-winter climate. When you place the rosebush on the cone, fan the roots over the cone's surface. Holding the rose in position, fill in the hole with the soil, constantly tamping it firmly around the roots. ¶ Start a hose trickling at the edge of the hole and continue to let it run until the soil is satu- ✒

'Just Joey'
Hybrid tea rose
Apricot
2 to 3 feet high
Fragrance: significant
Bloom: repeated

❧

What You Need
1 bare-root 'Just Joey' rosebush
3 square feet of prepared
ground with at least
4 hours full sun
Small pruning clippers
Balanced rose fertilizer

❧

When to Buy
Bare-root, winter or early
spring from mail-order catalogues and
nurseries (potted, spring through
summer from nurseries)

❧

When to Plant
Bare-root, late winter or spring
(potted, spring through summer)

❧

rated and has settled. Add more soil if necessary. Keep well watered thereafter, maintaining a moist root zone during the period of growth and bloom. ¶ Fertilize after leaves have appeared and every three to four weeks afterward, with a balanced rose fertilizer. Stop fertilizing in approximately early September in areas with mild-winter climates, late July in areas with cold-winter climates. Begin fertilizing again when bushes begin to emerge from dormancy. In late winter or early spring, when the bushes are dormant and the buds have just begun to swell, remove inward-facing growth and crossing branches. Cut back the bush to three or four main branches, making each cut about $1/4$ inch above an outward-facing bud.

A WALKWAY GARDEN

The small, often narrow span of open ground between a walkway and a wall is a welcoming location for roses. The wall can be used to provide support for shrubs or for climbers, as well as accommodating large-growing species roses. A graceful hybrid perpetual rose, such as 'American Beauty' (also called 'Madame Ferdinand Jamin') and a species rose such as Rosa roxburghii—a combination delighting the rose enthusiast with a visual slice of rose history—can be dramatically juxtaposed in the space defined by a walkway. A successful and satisfying walkway rose garden might equally consist of a collection of miniature roses, a selection of several rosebushes, or an orderly row of tree roses, depending upon the nature and the passions of the gardener. ¶ **HOW TO DO IT** ¶ Choose a location with at least four hours of full sun. Dig a hole for each rosebush approximately 1½ feet across and 1½ feet deep, spacing them at least 3 feet apart. Use pruning clippers to cut off any broken or bruised roots ½ inch above the break or bruise. Cut back each branch by one-third, to ¼ inch above an outward-facing bud. Submerge the roots in a bucket of water for an hour or two or as long as twenty-four hours before planting. ¶ To plant, refill each hole with some of the loose soil, mounding it in the shape of a cone. The cones should be sufficiently tall that the rosebushes, when set upon them, can have the roots be well covered with soil and the bud union, if there is one, can be situated 2 inches above the soil line if planted in a mild-winter climate or 2 inches below in a cold-winter climate. When you place each rosebush on a cone, fan the roots over the cone's surface. Holding the rose in position, fill in the hole with the soil. Repeat. ¶ Start a hose trickling at the edge of one of the holes and continue to let it run until the soil is saturated and has settled, before switching it to the other hole. Add more soil if necessary. ✦

'American Beauty'
Hybrid perpetual rose
Red
6 to 8 feet high
Fragrance: intense
Bloom: repeated

❧

Rosa roxburghii
Species rose
Pink
8 to 12 feet high
Fragrance: medium
Bloom: repeated

❧

What You Need
*1 bare-root 'American Beauty' and
1 Rosa roxburghii rosebush
6 square feet of prepared ground
with at least 4 hours direct sun
Small pruning clippers
Balanced rose fertilizer*

❧

When to Buy
*Bare-root, winter or early spring from
mail-order catalogues or specialty nurseries
(potted, spring through summer from
specialty nurseries)*

❧

When to Plant
*Bare-root, late winter or early spring
(potted, spring through summer)*

❧

Keep well watered thereafter, maintaining moist root zones during the period of growth and bloom. ¶ Fertilize after leaves have appeared and every three to four weeks afterward, with a balanced rose fertilizer. Stop fertilizing in approximately early September in areas with mild-winter climates, late July in areas with cold-winter climates. Begin fertilizing again when bushes begin to emerge from dormancy. ¶ In late winter or early spring, when the bushes are dormant and the buds have just begun to swell, cut away from 'American Beauty' any dead wood, inward-growing or crossing branches, and side shoots. Cut back branches to reduce the bush size by one-third, making each cut about $1/4$ inch above an outward-facing bud. For *R. roxburghii*, prune by removing any dead wood and cutting back canes as desired, to shape.

CLIMBERS

AND RAMBLERS

FOR TRELLISES

AND VAST

COVER

I confess that my heart belongs to climbers and ramblers. I have always been enthralled by the sight of masses of roses growing in great mounds, winding up and around balconies, crossing roofs, or sprawling over fences or abandoned buildings. Few vistas are more inviting than an arch or pergola covered with roses signaling the entrance to a house or a garden, unless it is that of a trellised wall protected by a profusion of canes and blooms, or a tree embraced by snaking rose canes. ❧ Climbers and ramblers have much in common but some significant differences as well. They belong to many different categories of roses, and hence we find hybrid tea climbers as well as species climbers, rambling species, perpetual hybrid ramblers, and so forth. Ramblers generally flower only once during the year, and their flowers are smallish. Climbers are more often repeat flowering and the blooms are medium to large. Climbers tend to be more constrained, even stiff, in their growing habit and to develop woody trunks. Ramblers on the other hand have a wild, loose growth pattern wherein they send up numerous shoots from the base of the bush. These shoots may be thirty feet or more in length, reaching up and out and over whatever is nearby. Ramblers require little pruning and are best left to their own wandering devices. ❧ Props for climbers and ramblers include arbors, trellises, pergolas—open structures of some depth—trees, rooftops, and windowsills. Ramblers in particular, left on their own without a prop, will create huge mounds that are very dramatic in a setting that can contain them.

'GOLDEN SHOWERS' ON A GREEN PERGOLA

Quick-growing, sturdy, robust, undemanding, repeating its bloom from spring into fall, this is a truly reliable rose. It has a reaching, spreading habit, and it embraces the five-foot wide, seven-foot tall green wooden pergola where I grow it. Not only does it make a welcoming entryway as it arches over the top of the pergola, I can count on cutting a goodly number of blooms from it almost every day throughout the seasons. ¶ **HOW TO DO IT** ¶ Choose a location with at least four hours of full sun. Install or construct the pergola. Dig a hole approximately 1½ feet across and 1½ deep and 1 foot distant from the middle of one side of the pergola. ¶ Use pruning clippers to cut off any broken or bruised roots ½ inch above the break or bruise. Cut away any weak, broken, or crossing branches. Cut back each branch by one-third, to ¼ inch above an outward-facing bud. Submerge the roots in a bucket of water for an hour or two or as long as twenty-four hours before planting. ¶ To plant, refill the holes with some of the loose soil, mounding it in the shape of a cone. The cone should be sufficiently tall that the rosebush, when set upon it, can have the roots well covered with soil and the bud union, if there is one, can be situated 2 inches above the soil line if planted in a mild-winter climate or 2 inches below in a cold-winter climate. When you place the rosebush on the cone, fan the roots over the cone's surface. Holding the rose in position, fill in the rest of the hole with the soil, constantly tamping it firmly around the roots. Start a hose trickling at the edge of the hole and continue to let it run until the soil is saturated and has settled, adding more soil if necessary. Keep well watered thereafter, maintaining moisture in the root zone during the season of growth and bloom. ¶ Fertilize after leaves have appeared and every three to four weeks afterward, ✁

'Golden Showers'
Floribunda climbing rose
Yellow
8 to 12 feet high
Fragrance: medium
Bloom: repeated

❧

What You Need
1 bare-root climbing
'Golden Showers' rosebush
5 square feet of prepared ground with
at least 4 hours full sun
Small pruning clippers
Purchased or constructed pergola
Balanced rose fertilizer
Gardener's tape

❧

When to Buy
Bare-root, winter or early spring from
mail-order catalogues or nurseries (potted,
spring through summer from nurseries)

❧

When to Plant
Bare-root, late winter or early spring
(potted, spring through summer)

❧

with a balanced rose fertilizer. Stop fertilizing in approximately early September in areas with mild-winter climates, late July in areas with cold-winter climates. Begin fertilizing again when bushes begin to emerge from dormancy. ¶ To train the rose to climb the pergola, use gardener's tape to tie the canes to the pergola walls and rails, and eventually across the top. ¶ Keep spent blooms removed to encourage new blooms. In late winter or early spring when the buds have begun to swell, prune by cutting away any dead growth and any crossing or inward-facing branches. Cut back each cane by one-quarter to one-third, to $\frac{1}{4}$ inch above an outward-facing bud, and then cut back the side shoots, where blooms occur, to 2 to 3 inches.

A CLASSIC BANKSIA ROSE

Some summer, driving down the streets of a small town or along a country lane almost anywhere in America, you have probably seen a mass of yellow blossoms covering a roof, climbing entwined in a tree, or winding over a barn. Small double, intensely fragrant, pale yellow blossoms that blanket long canes—40 feet and more long—are the identifying feature of this wild rose, whose origins are in central and western China. There it grows freely along the banks of rivers and down roadsides, as well as in ancient gardens. ¶ A cultivated version of the wild rose, the banksia variety 'Lutea' is quite easy to locate in nurseries. Plant it where it can spread and climb and show itself off, extending the hint and memory of its exotic origins. ¶ **HOW TO DO IT** ¶ Choose a location with at least four hours of full sun and adequate rambling space. Dig a hole approximately 1 1/2 feet across, 1 1/2 feet deep, and 1 to 1 1/2 feet out from a wall, tree, or other climbable structure. Buy a trellis, or build a simple one as follows. Attach three or four lengths of strong wire to a sturdy stake driven into the ground behind where the rose will be planted and attach the loose ends of the wire firmly to the eaves of the roof or other structure. Use pruning clippers to cut off any broken or bruised roots 1/2 inch above the break or bruise. Submerge the roots in a bucket of water for an hour or two or as long as twenty-four hours before planting. ¶ To plant, refill the holes with some of the loose soil, mounding it in the shape of a cone. The cone should be sufficiently tall that the rosebush, when set upon it, can have the roots well covered with soil and the bud union, if there is one, can be situated 2 inches above the soil line if planted in a mild-winter climate or 2 inches below in a cold-winter climate. When you place the rosebush on the cone, fan the roots over the cone's surface. Holding the rose in position, fill in the rest of the hole with the soil, constantly tamping it firmly around the roots. Start a hose trickling at ✐

'Lutea'
Rosa banksia *species climbing rose*
Pale yellow
20 to 40 feet high or long
Fragrance: intense
Bloom: once
❧

When You Need
1 bare-root 'Lutea' banksia rosebush
Small pruning clippers
*12 square feet of prepared ground with
at least 4 hours full sun*
Purchased trellis or wire and stake
Balanced rose fertilizer
Gardener's tape
❧

When to Buy
*Bare-root, winter or early spring from
mail-order catalogues or nurseries (potted,
spring through summer from nurseries)*
❧

When to Plant
*Bare-root, late winter or spring
(potted, spring through summer)*
❧

the edge of the hole and continue to let it run until the soil is saturated and has settled, adding more soil if necessary. Keep well watered thereafter, maintaining a moist root zone until the rose is established. ¶ In the first year, apply a balanced rose fertilizer after leaves have appeared and every three to four weeks afterward during the season of growth and bloom. Over two or three years, decrease the frequency of fertilizing to twice yearly, in spring before budding and in summer when bloom has finished. Stop fertilizing in approximately early September in areas with mild-winter climates, late July in areas with cold-winter climates. Begin fertilizing again when bushes begin to emerge from dormancy. ¶ When the bloom has finished in summer, remove any dead wood and, if desired to shape and control growth, cut back the canes.

'QUEEN ELIZABETH' ATOP AN ARBOR

Imagine having morning coffee outside on a balcony or deck, seated next to a fragrant sea of deep pink roses. The roses grow and bloom throughout the summer along the uppermost surface of an arbor that extends outward from floor level, creating a spectacular framework. Although not a proper climber, it grows so tall and upright it may be treated like one, especially in areas with mild-winter climates. ¶ The rose stems, once the bush is trained onto the arbor, naturally grow upward toward the light rather than downward into the shade. To cut the roses for bouquets, lean out across the railing of the balcony or deck and snip them with your clippers, or cut those that grow along the outer sides of the arbor. ¶ **HOW TO DO IT** ¶ Choose a location with at least four hours of full sun. Install or construct the arbor. Dig two holes, each approximately 1½ feet across, 1½ feet deep, and 1 foot distant from the middle of an end wall of the arbor. ¶ Use pruning clippers to cut off any broken or bruised roots ½ inch above the break or bruise, and cut away any weak, broken, or crossing branches. Cut each branch back by one-third, to ¼ inch above an outward-facing bud. Submerge the roots in a bucket of water for an hour or two or as long as twenty-four hours before planting. ¶ To plant, refill each hole with some of the loose soil, mounding it in the shape of a cone. The cone should be sufficiently tall that the rosebush, when set upon it, can have the roots well covered with soil and the bud union, if there is one, can be situated 2 inches above the soil line if planted in a mild-winter climate or 2 inches below in a cold-winter climate. When you place each rosebush on one of the cones, fan the roots over the cone's surface. Holding the rose in position, fill in the rest of the hole with the soil, constantly tamping it firmly around the roots. Start a hose trickling at the edge of the hole and continue to let it run until the soil is saturated and has settled, adding more soil if necessary. Keep ✒

'Queen Elizabeth'
Grandiflora rose
Pink
10 to 12 feet high
Fragrance: medium
Bloom: repeated

❧

What You Need
2 bare-root 'Queen Elizabeth' rosebushes
6-foot by 2-foot area of prepared ground
with at least 4 hours full sun
Small pruning clippers
Purchased or constructed arbor
Balanced rose fertilizer
Gardener's tape

❧

When to Buy
Bare-root, winter or early spring from
mail-order catalogues or nurseries (potted,
spring through summer from nurseries)

❧

When to Plant
Bare-root, late winter or early spring
(potted, spring through summer)

❧

well watered thereafter, maintaining moisture in the root zone during the period of growth and bloom. ¶ Fertilize after leaves have appeared and every three to four weeks afterward, with a balanced rose fertilizer. Stop fertilizing in approximately early September in areas with mild-winter climates, late July in areas with cold-winter climates. Begin fertilizing again when bushes begin to emerge from dormancy. ¶ To train the rose to climb the trellised walls of the arbor, use gardener's tape to tie the canes to the arbor walls and eventually across the top. ¶ In late winter or early spring when the buds have begun to swell, prune by cutting away any dead growth and any crossing or inward-facing branches. Cut back each cane by one-quarter to one-third, to $1/4$ inch above an outward-facing bud, shaping as desired.

A rambler to entwine a tree

This is a dreamscape of roses and it came, unbeknownst to me for months, with the abandoned house we bought. When I first saw the nondescript thornless green shrub growing stubbornly next to a forlorn crape myrtle tree along the dusty drive, it was about three feet high and as wide. We watered the rosebush more out of curiosity than anything else. It soared that first year, sending out canes five, six, even seven feet long that began to snake up the tree. The following April it burst forth in clouds of deep pink buds followed by pastel poofs of fragrant blossoms. As we watered along the drive, other roses once planted there began to reappear. Now, great mounding shrubs on both sides of the crape myrtle send canes thirty feet high to climb and curl among the branches of the tree. The roses begin to bloom just as the tree is leafing out. In full bloom the whole presents a huge mass of pink that can be seen a mile away. ¶ **HOW TO DO IT** ¶ Choose a location with at least four hours of full sun. It must offer room for the rose to spread and climb the tree, which can be living or dead. Dig a hole approximately 1½ feet across, 1½ feet deep, and 3 to 5 feet away from the tree. Use pruning clippers to cut off any broken or bruised roots ½ inch above the break or bruise. Cut away any crossing branches. Submerge the roots in a bucket of water for an hour or two or as long as twenty-four hours before planting. ¶ To plant the rosebush, refill the hole with some of the loose soil, mounding it in the shape of a cone. The cone should be sufficiently tall that the rosebush, when set upon it, can have the roots well covered with soil. When you place the rosebush on the cone, fan the roots over the cone's surface. Holding the rose in position, fill in the hole with the soil, constantly tamping it firmly around the roots. ✒

'Adelaide d'Orléans' or similar
Sempervirens *hybrid*
rambling rose
Pale pink
15 to 30 feet high
Fragrance: significant
Bloom: once in late spring or
early summer, perhaps
❧

What You Need
1 bare-root 'Adelaide d'Orléans' rosebush
1 tree, either evergreen or deciduous
20 square feet of prepared ground with
at least 4 hours full sun
Small pruning clippers
Balanced rose fertilizer
❧

When to Buy
Bare-root, winter or early spring from
mail-order catalogues or specialty nurseries
(potted, spring through summer from
specialty nurseries)
❧

When to Plant
Bare-root, late winter or early spring
(potted, spring through summer)
❧

Start a hose trickling at the edge of the hole and continue to let it run until the soil is saturated and has settled, adding more soil if necessary. Keep well watered thereafter, maintaining a moist root zone throughout the period of growth and bloom. ¶ In the first year apply a balanced rose fertilizer after the rose has leafed out and every three or four weeks afterward, during the season of growth and bloom. Over two to three years decrease the frequency of fertilizing to twice yearly, in spring before budding and in summer when bloom has finished. ¶ As the canes grow, they will find their way to the nearby tree. ¶ In summer, when the bloom is finished, cut away dead wood from the base of the bush if desired for a cleaner look. Also if desired, in some years, cut back the bushes to shape them.

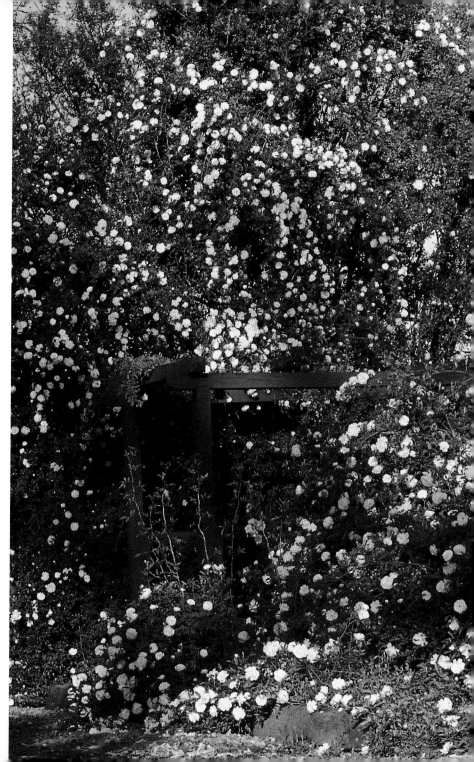

ROSE
GARDENS

lthough "rose garden" brings to mind immediately a formal, large planting, a rose garden may be as simple as one or two bushes spread against a wall, as small as a collection in cache-pots on a balcony or patio, or as rampant as an overflow of roses onto trees and fences. ❧ The focus of a rose garden might be only miniature roses or only old roses, or it might be the contrast of old and modern, shrubs and climbers. Its setting can weave in other flowers as well, and these may be of the same size, soaring above the roses, or growing in a carpet beneath them. ❧ A rose garden is in the heart and eye of its gardener.

A ROSE CIRCLE

Geometrical and dramatic, yet simple, this rose circle garden encompasses multiples of hybrid tea roses, floribundas, grandifloras, and English roses in complementary shades of yellow, cream, amber, pink, and red. All the roses are repeat bloomers and provide lively color from spring through fall. The border and pathways are constructed of river rocks, but brick, flagstone, or other rocks could be used with equal success. Feathery, silver-leafed dusty miller lines the inner side of the stone circle, softening the border and highlighting the colors of the roses. The center ornament provides a focus for the garden. ¶ Although other roses could be used in a garden of this type, hybrid teas, at least one grandiflora, floribundas, and certain new English roses lend themselves to the pruning and shaping that gives a small, geometrical garden a defining sense of controlled and harmonious order. Among a number of alternative silver-white border plantings are artemisia and sweet allysum. ¶ **HOW TO DO IT** ¶ Choose a location with at least 4 hours of full sun. In the center of the prepared circle of ground, draw another circle 4 feet in diameter. Lay out the remaining garden design using small stakes and twine. Divide the ground outside the inner circle into quadrants. Draw two lines on each side of the quadrant lines 1 foot from the line to make four pathways, each 2 feet wide. Finally, draw a line 1½ feet in from the outer circle edge to make an area for the border, and place optional pathway and border materials and center ornament. ¶ Allow six roses for each quadrant, spacing them evenly in three rows; one of three rosebushes, one of two, and one of one. Dig a hole 1½ feet in diameter and 1½ feet deep for each rose. To plant, water, fertilize, and prune, follow the directions for 'Just Joey' on pages 68-69.

Hybrid tea roses: pink 'Dainty Bess', 'Duet', 'Sheer Bliss', 'Sonia'; reddish-pink 'Color Magic'; yellow 'Gold Medal'
Grandiflora rose: pink 'Tournament of Roses'
Floribunda roses: yellow 'Sunsprite'; apricot 'Amber Queen'; red 'Trumpeter'; pink 'Sexy Rexy'
English roses: white 'Perdita'; pink 'Heritage'; yellow 'Graham Thomas'
Heights: as shown
Fragrance: most, scented
Bloom: for all named above, repeated

❧

What You Need
24 of the above-named rosebushes, bare-root, or other similar hybrid tea, floribunda, and English roses
Border plants (optional)
A circle 25 feet in diameter of prepared ground with at least 4 hours full sun
Small pruning clippers
Balanced rose fertilizer
Stones, brick, or other pathway and border materials (optional)
Center ornament such as an urn or sundial

❧

When to Buy
Bare-root, winter or early spring from mail-order catalogues or specialty nurseries (potted, spring through summer from specialty nurseries)

❧

When to Plant
Bare-root, late winter or early spring (potted, spring through summer)

❧

Rose garden along a fence

A simple chainlink or other fence is transformed into a flowing wave of color and fragrance by a mixture of old and new roses planted along its length. Red, pink, and white blooms mingle, some of them large and gracefully bending like those of 'Belle of Portugal', others small like those of 'Cinderella', as the canes twist and overlap in this splendidly rampant display of the beauty of the rose. Once planted and underway, these roses need no further care than adequate water and the cutting back of dead wood every few years. ¶ A rose garden of this type is ideal for a country or weekend house where one wants to enjoy roses but cannot commit to a lot of nurturing. Some of the selections here are once-blooming, others are continual or repeat bloomers. ¶ **HOW TO DO IT** ¶ Choose a location with at least four hours of full sun, along a sturdy fence. Divide the length of the fence into equal segments, in this case, eight segments each 5 feet long. In the center of each segment dig a hole 2 feet from the fence, 1½ feet wide, and 1½ feet deep. Plant, water, and fertilize as directed for 'Adelaide d'Orléans' on pages 80-81. Let the roses follow their own form for two or three years, then, if desired after bloom is finished, cut away any dead wood underneath.

Modern shrub rose: pink
'Sperrieshoop'
Species rose:
pink *Rosa canina* (dog rose)
Gallica roses: pink 'Complicata',
'La Mortola', 'Cocktail', 'Climbing
Cinderella', 'Dr. Huey'
Heights: as shown
Fragrance: most, scented
Bloom: period varies

What You Need
8 bare-root rosebushes, the
above-named or other similar roses
40 feet of fence
40 foot by 4 foot area of prepared
ground with at least four hours full sun
Small pruning clippers
Balanced rose fertilizer

When to Buy
Bare-root, winter or early spring from
mail-order catalogues and specialty
nurseries (potted, spring through summer
from specialty nurseries)

When to Plant
Bare-root, late winter or spring
(potted, spring through summer)

A CURBSIDE GARDEN

A small space bordering a curb is nevertheless space enough for a garden of thirteen old and new roses. A lush hybrid musk climber is even accommodated by planting it at the corner of the bungalow and training along the roofline, beneath the eaves. There, the bush and its blooms frame the windows, and its rich scent can waft inside when the windows are open. Tidily shaped and pruned fragrant rose tree standards are at window level, where they fit into the small setting without dominating it, and in a third layer of planting, orderly rows of rosebushes are neatly separated from the curb by a low, clipped hedge of boxwood. ¶ **HOW TO DO IT** ¶ Choose a location with at least four hours of full sun. Making each rose site a hole 1½ feet deep and 1½ feet wide, position the climbing rose 2 feet from a wall with a window. The climbing rose should be 3 to 4 feet away from the site for the nearest rose tree. In a row nearest the house, site each rose tree and one of the repeat-blooming roses, equidistantly spaced. In a row 3 feet distant from the first, plant the remaining repeat-blooming rosebushes slightly offset from the first row and equidistantly spaced. In a third row 3 feet from the second, site each of the floribunda rosebushes spaced the same as the first row. Plant, water, and fertilize, and prune the rosebushes, except for the pruning of the rose trees and the climbers, as directed for 'Just Joey' on pages 68-69. ¶ At the same time as pruning the rosebushes, prune the branches of the rose trees by removing inward-facing growth and crossing branches. Reduce the number to three or four main branches, and cut back the branches by one-third, making each cut ¼ inch above an outward-facing bud. ¶ For the climber, follow the planting, watering, fertilizing, and pruning directions for 'Mermaid' on pages 66-67. ¶ Plant and care for the boxwood hedge according to directions provided by your nursery.

English rose: pink 'Hero'
Floribunda rose: white 'Iceberg'
Hybrid musk climbing rose:
pale yellow 'Buff Beauty'
Hybrid tea roses: white 'Frau Karl
Druschki'; creamy yellow
'Belle Blonde'
Hybrid tea rose tree:
pink 'Sweet Surrender'
Heights: as shown
Fragrance: most, scented
Bloom: repeated

❧

What You Need
13 roses, the above named or others of their
types: 1 hybrid musk climber,
3 tree standards, 4 floribunda bushes,
5 repeat-blooming bushes
Boxwood or other hedgeplant (optional)
20 by 15 foot area of prepared ground
with at least 4 hours full sun
1 purchased trellis or wire and stake
Small pruning clippers
Balanced rose fertilizer
Gardener's tape

❧

When to Buy
Bare-root, winter or early spring from
mail-order catalogues or specialty nurseries
(potted, spring through summer
from specialty nurseries)

❧

When to Plant
Bare-root, late winter or early spring
(potted, spring through summer)

❧

ROSES AND CACTUS

Although roses do require abundant water, the area around them may remain quite arid, allowing a garden that mixes roses with cactus or other drought-resistant plants. A single rosebush, perhaps a climbing one, is enough to make a dramatic garden and keep watering responsibilities to a minimum. Any types of roses might be used, ranging from species roses to hybrid teas. The important consideration in a garden that combines water-loving plants with those that readily suffer from overwatering is to have a watering scheme that allows for plant needs, such as a combination of drip and handwatering rather than overhead sprinkling. ¶ If you choose a climbing rose, such as 'Renae', a natural look can be achieved by allowing the dead wood beneath to remain untrimmed, thus building up a structure underneath the rosebush for the new growth to climb upon. Pruning is then reduced to once every few years. Alternatively, provide a structure, such as a tree or pillar, for the rose to climb. ¶ **HOW TO DO IT** ¶ Choose a location with at least four hours of full sun. Dig a hole 1½ feet in diameter and 1½ feet deep. Plant the rose, and also water, fertilize, and prune, as specified for Rose Garden along a Fence on pages 87-88. ¶ Intersperse the area of the garden around the rose with cactus, and care for them according to directions provided by your nursery.

'Renae'
Polyantha climbing rose
Pink
10 to 15 feet high
Fragrance: intense
Bloom: repeated

What You Need
1 bare-root 'Renae' rosebush
Cactus or other drought-tolerant plants
10 by 15 foot area of prepared ground
with at least 4 hours full sun
Small pruning clippers
Balanced rose fertilizer

When to Buy
Bare-root, winter or early spring from
mail-order catalogues or specialty nurseries
(potted, spring through summer from
specialty nurseries)

When to Plant
Bare-root, late winter or early spring
(potted, spring through summer)

FROM YOUR

GARDEN

One of the most substantive delights of growing roses is the luxury of cutting and gathering them, whether for your own uses or to give to others. The bounty of roses is greater than simply the flowers, since throughout the year the ever-changing bush has something to offer. In spring the first flush of leaves is burgundy and mahogany, bronze and varying shades of green, some of them pointed and some rounded, smooth or ruffly—special tokens to tie onto gifts, garnish a tart or cake, or add to a nosegay of pansies or violets. Blossoms and buds of early bloomers can be tucked into May baskets. ❧ Come the first plump buds of later spring and early summer, you can cut armloads from the bushes without diminishing their outdoor display. In full summer the munificence is enough for bouquets in every room, garlands as gifts, and even for wedding cake decoration or to send overnight across the country. ❧ As summer turns to fall and winter, the rose hips give a glorious and varied display to bring inside as well as to admire outside. At pruning time in late winter or early spring, take a cutting of one of your roses and root it to pass on, and impart to the receiver of your gift a continuity of beauty.

OVERNIGHT ROSES

I never left my mother-in-law's house in summer without an armload of roses from her garden. She wrapped them in newspaper after cutting them, then soaked the paper in water before wrapping the whole in waxed paper to keep the bouquet fresh during the hour-long drive home. As soon as I arrived, I put the roses in a vase, and throughout the week they reminded me of her. ¶ Not only can we send visiting friends home with roses from our gardens, with the efficiency of guaranteed one-day overnight mail services, we can give roses from our gardens to friends and family who live hundreds, even thousands of miles away, for any occasion—even to set a wedding table. The best time to do this is in spring, early summer, or fall, when there is the least risk of your package being exposed to too much heat. Choose roses that are still in bud, but whose outer layer or two of petals have unfurled. ¶ **HOW TO DO IT** ¶ To condition the roses for shipping, let them stand overnight in a bucket with enough water to reach three-quarters of the way up the stems. ¶ To pack the roses, first wrap them loosely in four or five layers of moist paper towels, then in two layers of waxed paper. Loosely wrap the whole with two layers of newspaper to provide additional insulation. Finally, fasten bubble wrap around the newspaper; slip this into the addressed overnight mailer along with a note or card, and send it off. It is a good idea to alert the person to whom you are sending the roses to expect the delivery and give an approximate time, if possible. ¶ Note: Verify with Federal Express, UPS, or the U.S. Postal Service that the destination to which you are shipping is one to which they will guarantee overnight delivery.

What You Need
6 to 8 stems of budding
roses from your garden
Bucket
Paper towels
Waxed paper
Newspaper
Bubblewrap
Addressed box mailer for priority
overnight Federal Express,
UPS, or U.S. Postal
Service delivery

WEDDING CAKE ROSES

What You Need
Rosebuds and blooms
Bucket
1 cup confectioner's sugar
Cake
¼ cup milk
Toothpicks cut neatly in half

All flowery cakes, but especially wedding cakes laden with precisely shaped roses made of tinted icing, fascinate me. I even once bought a rather elaborate cake-decorating set with complete instructions, but the results of my efforts fell short of what I saw in my mind's eye. Consequently, I was quite delighted to discover that it was not only acceptable but considered très elegant to decorate cakes with fresh rosebuds, petals, full blossoms, leaves, even rose hips. Candied ones can be used as well, of course, but fresh ones have a very different look. ¶ Do be sure to use only roses, leaves, and hips that you know have not been treated with a chemical spray, as roses are among the tastiest of edible flowers. ¶ **HOW TO DO IT** ¶ Condition the roses overnight in a bucket of water deep enough to reach three-quarters of the way up the stems. ¶ Put the sugar in a bowl and add the milk a little at a time to make a thin paste. ¶ As close as possible to presentation time, decorate the cake with the roses in one of two ways, depending upon where you want to place the roses. If on a flat surface, simply cut off the stem of the rose, then place a dab of the sugar paste on the back and gently press the rose to the cake. If the rose will be on a vertical surface, cut off its stem and insert a toothpick through its base. Gently push the toothpick into the cake, fixing the rose in place.

Rose hip bouquets

Rose hips, or heps, as they are also called, are the casings that hold the rose seeds. The hips of roses vary in number, size, color, and shape. Some, like those of the rugosas, are quite prominent, while others, such as many hybrid teas', are negligible. ¶ The hips of the species roses are outstanding in both shape and color and make gorgeously wild wreaths. I often cut long canes from those in my garden and keep them in bouquets throughout the winter, adding seasonal flowers, such as narcissus. ¶ **HOW TO DO IT** ¶ Cut the rose canes with the clippers at the base of the bush, if they grow from there, or if they do not then cut about ¼ inch above branching points. Once canes are cut, put them in a vase or other container with about 6 inches of water in the bottom. As the water evaporates, the hips will slowly dry. ¶ If you want to add fresh flowers to the rose hips, fill the container about half full with water. When the fresh flowers have died, discard the water.

What You Need
5 to 7 canes of rose hips,
each at least 18 inches long
Small pruning clippers or shears
Vase or other container
Water
Fresh flowers, if desired

MAY BASKETS

When I was a child, Hallmark cards published a punch-out book of May baskets that my mother helped me construct, and early on the first day of May we went out into the garden together and filled them with sweet peas, geraniums, bougainvillea, and daisies. I made a quick round of deliveries, hanging flower-filled baskets on the neighbors' doors. It was an exciting and secretive experience, one I have often thought about with pleasure, and I have begun to repeat it. It is just as much fun now, though in a different way, as it was when I was a child. ¶ The custom itself is an ancient one dating to pagan times along with Maypoles and dances to celebrate spring. It had a great vogue during the late 1800s and well into the first half of this century. I am happy to see the custom enjoying a revival as we near the end of the millenium, marking a continuity with the past. ¶ **HOW TO DO IT** ¶ Fit each basket with a waterproof container. The container should fit the basket without tipping over or falling to one side. Fill the container half full of water. Arrange the flowers and foliage you cut in the baskets. ¶ Tie a ribbon on each basket and, if desired, a tag with the name of the person to whom you are giving it.

What You Need
6 baskets, small or large
6 waterproof containers such
as wax-coated cups or tubs,
in sizes to fit the baskets
Cut roses and other flowers and foliage,
such as tulips, lilacs, and ivy,
enough to fill six baskets
Ribbon
Tags, if desired
❧

Rooted cuttings to give

Many of the old roses we see growing throughout the country were first brought here by immigrants who carried precious cuttings of beloved roses from their homelands. When the cuttings were planted and the roses flourished and bloomed, the new homes were made familiar and the past became linked with the future. ¶ Although we have many nurseries today where we can purchase any number of roses, there remains something special about preparing a cutting oneself, and then watching it root and grow. It provides the sense of accomplishment that comes only from doing something from scratch, like baking bread or building a bookcase. ¶ Many, many roses are easy and quick to root from cuttings, but others may be stubborn. Only experimentation will reveal whether your roses will readily root. Be patient and enjoy the adventure. Do be forewarned that most recent modern roses are patented, and that reproduction of them is illegal. If in doubt, check with the American Rose Society whether the rose you want to root and reproduce is patented. ¶ There are a number of methods by which to induce cuttings to root. Rooting hormone, which is readily available at nurseries and garden centers, stimulates root growth, but successful rooting can be achieved without using it. ¶ **HOW TO DO IT** ¶ Remove the leaves from the lengths of rose canes. Select on each two adjacent nodes, which will be the basis for your cutting. Using the clippers, cut off the top about ¹/₄ inch above the upper node, and discard; cut the bottom end on a long diagonal to provide maximum surface for rooting. Leave as much stem on the cutting as possible beneath the lower node. ¶ If you use rooting hormone, dip the diagonal surface into it. Place the cutting in the prepared ground, diagonal end down, leaving the two nodes above the surface. Water the ground thoroughly. If desired, place a Mason or other glass jar or vented plastic bag over the cutting to help retain moisture and warmth, but prop up the bottom of it ✧

What You Need
1 or more 6-inch lengths of
postbloom rose cane with 4 or 5 nodes,
with or without leaves
Small pruning clippers
Rooting hormone (optional)
1 or more square feet prepared ground
receiving little or no direct sunlight
Plastic bag or Mason jar (optional)
❧

with a block or stone during the day to allow air circulation. If you use either, be careful not to bump the cutting or otherwise disturb the root growth as you move the jar or bag. Alternatively, the cutting may be planted in a container filled with a mixture of potting soil and sand. ¶ Two important points about growing roses from cuttings are that the ground and root zone must be kept moist at all times and the roots must not be disturbed while they are first growing. ¶ Once the cutting has leafed out, and at least two inches of new growth have appeared, you may transfer the now-rooted cutting to a container or to its permanent garden location.

Resources

Mail-order Nurseries

Antique Rose Emporium
Route 5, Box 143
Brenham, TX 77833
Tel: (409) 836-9051
Fax: (409) 836-0928
Good selection of old roses grown on their own roots. Catalogue: $5.00

Garden Valley Ranch
498 Pepper Road
Mail to: P.O. Box 750953
Petaluma, CA 94962
Tel: (707) 795-0919
Owned by Ray Reddell, one of the largest whole-sale shippers in the U.S. of cut garden roses. Excellent selection of hybrid tea and floribunda roses. Catalogue: free

Heritage Rose Gardens
40350 Wilderness Road
Branscom, CA 95417
Tel: (707) 964-3748
Owned by rosarian Joyce Demits. Good selection of old roses and early modern roses grown on their own roots. Catalogue: $1.00

Hortico, Inc.
723 Robson Road
RR1, Waterdown
Ontario, Canada LOR 2H1
Tel: (905) 689-6984
Extensive listing of old and modern roses, including some difficult-to-find early modern roses and some that are found more commonly in the United Kingdom than the United States. Catalogue: $3.00

Mendocino Heirloom Roses
P.O. Box 670
Mendocino, CA 95460
Tel: (707) 877-1888 or (707) 937-0963
Owned by rosarians Gail Daly and Alice Flores. Good selection of old roses, plus some modern. Informative catalogue includes drought-resistant notations. Catalogue: $1.00

Rose Acres
6260 Fernwood Drive
Shingle Springs, CA 95682
Tel: (916) 626-1722
Owned by rosarian Muriel Humenick. Good selection of both old and modern roses, including miniatures. Catalogue: list free with SASE

Roses of Yesterday and Today
802 Brown's Valley Road
Watsonville, CA 95076-0398
Tel: (408) 724-3537
Fax: (800) 980-7673
Owned by rosarian Pat Wiley. Wide selection of old, unusual modern, and species roses. Most are budded onto rootstock. Catalogue considered a collector's item. Catalogue: $3.00

Royall River Roses (formerly
Forevergreen Farm)
70 New Gloucester Road
North Yarmouth, ME 04097
Tel: (207) 829-5830
Fax: (207) 829-6512
Owned by rosarian David King. Excellent selection of rugosa and other hardy roses, including species, old, and modern roses. Catalogue: $1.00

Sequoia Nursery
2519 E. Noble
Visalia, CA 93292
Tel: (209) 732-0190
Fax: (209) 732-0192
Owned by world-renowned rose breeder Ralph Moore, this nursery specializes in miniature and other modern roses bred by Mr. Moore, many of them interesting new introductions. It also has a good selection of old roses and early modern roses. Pot grown, most on their own roots. Wholesale and retail.

Vintage Gardens
2227 Gravenstein Highway South
Sebastopol, CA 95472
Tel: (707) 829-2035
Approximately 900 different roses, including old, exceptional modern, and species roses, some in limited supply. Catalogue: $4.00; free list

SOCIETIES AND ORGANIZATIONS

American Rose Society
Membership Secretary
P.O. Box 30,000
Shreveport, LA 71130
Prefers correspondence by mail.
Preeminent group for people interested in roses of all kinds.

Heritage Rose Foundation
1512 Gorman Street
Raleigh, NC 27606
Prefers correspondence by mail.
This foundation focuses on the preservation of old roses, including education and research about them.

The Heritage Roses Group
Started by noted California rosarian Miriam Wilkins in 1975, this is a nationwide fellowship of people interested in old roses who share information, gardens, and activities of all kinds. Membership is $5.00 a year. Please send a self-addressed, stamped envelope when corresponding with the co-ordinators.

Northeast United States
Lily Shohan
RD 1 Box 299
Clinton Corners, NY 12514

Northwest United States
Judy Dexter
23665 41st Street South
Kent, CA 98032

Southeast United States
Jan Wilson
1700 South Lafayette St.
Shelby, NC 28150

South Central States
Karen Walbrun
Route 2 Box 6661
Pipe Creek, TX 78063

Southwest States
(Last name beginning with A-G)
Betty L. Cooper
925 King Drive
El Cerrito, CA 94530
(Last name beginning with H-O)
Marlea Graham
100 Bear Oaks Drive
Martinez, CA 94553
(Last name beginning with P-Z)
Frances Grate
472 Gibson Avenue
Pacific Grove, CA 93940

BIBLIOGRAPHY

Austin, David.
Old Roses and English Roses.
Woodbridge, Suffolk, England:
Collector's Books, 1991.

_____.

Shrub Roses and Climbing Roses.
Woodbridge, Suffolk, England:
Collector's Books, 1993.

Christopher, Thomas.
In Search of Lost Roses.
New York: Summit Books, 1989.

Dobson, Beverly.
The Combined Rose List 1993.
New York: Beverly Dobson, 1993.

Joyce, David, and Brickell, Christopher.
*The Complete Guide to Pruning and
Training Plants.*
New York: Simon and Schuster, 1992.

McCann, Sean.
Miniature Roses: Their Care and Cultivation.
Harrisville, Pennsylvania: Stackpole
Books, 1991.

Moore, Ralph.
*The Breeding and Development of Modern
Moss Roses.*
Visalia, California: Moore-Sequoia,
no date.

Phillips, Roger, and Rix, Martyn.
The Random House Guide to Roses.
New York: Random House, 1988.

_____ .

"The Inheritance Factor," *Gardens Illustrated.*
October/November, 1993, page 68-73.

Reddell, Rayford Clayton.
Growing Good Roses.
Covelo, California: Yolla Bolly Press,
1988.

Index

Acknowledgments

Our editors Bill LeBlond and Leslie Jonath have been supportive and enthusiastic throughout as has our agent Susan Lescher. ¶ A special thanks to Jill Jacobson in the art department and to Aufuldish & Warinner for their design, and to Carey Charlesworth for editing and Hazel White for her expertise, and to Paula Tevis for her brilliant job of compiling and inputting. ¶ Numerous people shared their gardens, roses, memories, and expertise to make this book possible. We would especially like to thank: Gail Daly, Joyce Demits, John and Lisbeth Farmar-Bowers, Charlotte Glenn, Tom Carruth, Muriel Humenick, David Jeffery, Betty and Stuart Kimball, Bruce LeFaveur, Ralph Moore, Ethel Munson, Suzanne Portero, Ray Reddell, Warren Roberts, Jim Schrupp, Michaele Thunin, Miriam Wilkins. Also, Heritage Rose Society, Smith & Hawken, Sonoma Flower Company. —GB.

The gardeners I've met and the gardens I've visited have been inspirational! Thanks especially to John Dallas, Carol Grant, Lelain Crist of Floribunda, the Plante family, the Spielers, Trausen Vineyards, Newton Vineyard, Sutter Home, Camilla, Susan, Maggie, Kathy, Mary, Sandy, Joan, Ann, Betsy, Rick, John, Gary, and Julie (the ever-wonderful Wags) and sweet Bruce who is always willing to turn the car around in response to "Rose Alert."—FE